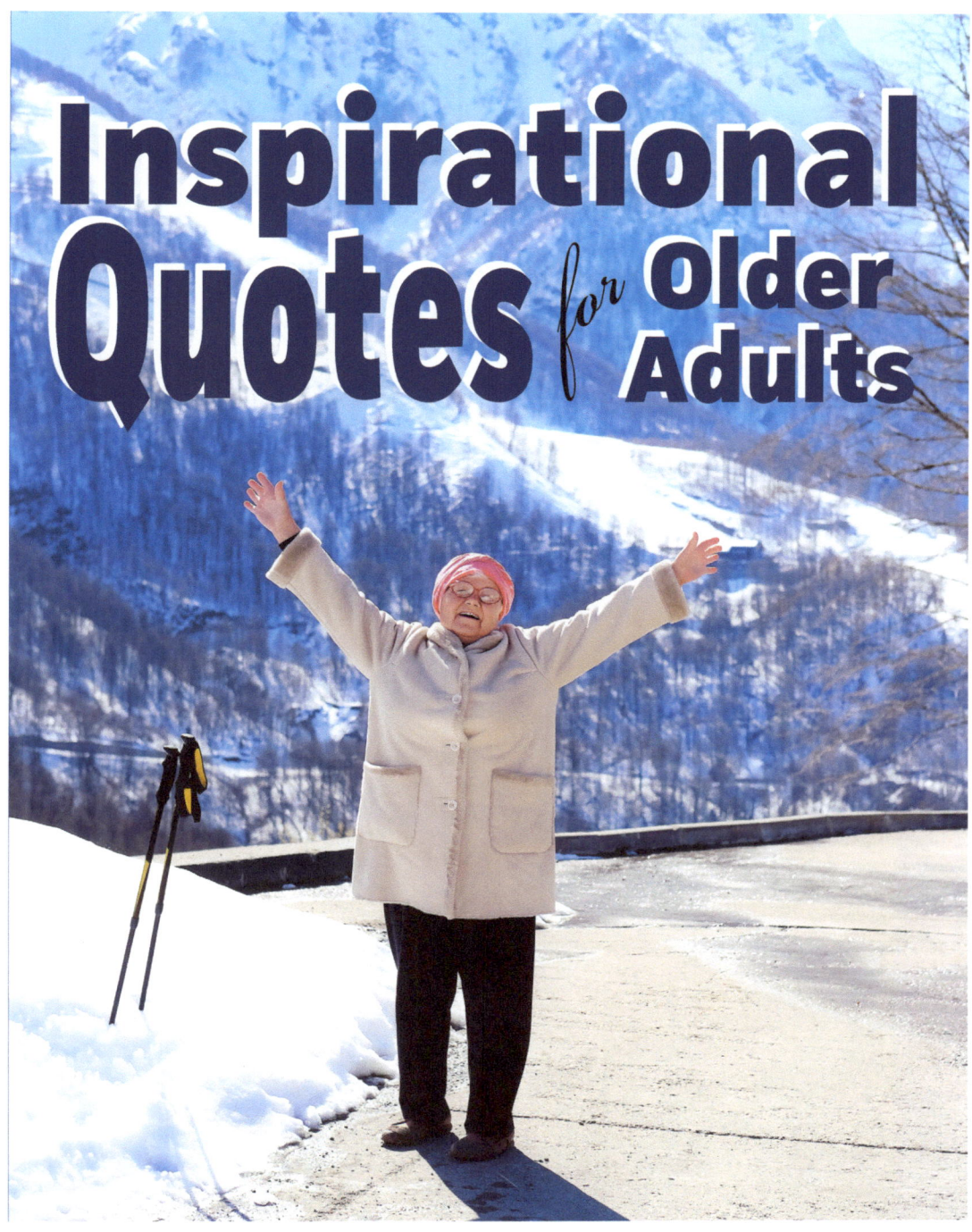

All rights reserved. This book or any portion thereof may not be reproduced or used in any manner whatsoever without the express written permission of the publisher except for the use of brief quotations in a book review.

Copyright © 2020 by Lasting Happiness
ISBN: 978-1-989842-03-4

A SHIP IN PORT IS SAFE

but

THAT IS NOT

what

SHIPS ARE BUILT FOR

DO what is RIGHT NOT what is EASY

EVERY FAILURE BRINGS WITH IT THE SEED OF AN EQUIVALENT SUCCESS

LIFE IS LIKE
riding a bicycle

TO KEEP YOUR BALANCE
YOU MUST KEEP MOVING

DON'T LOOK BACK

You're NOT GOING THAT WAY

It Starts With You

DO NOT LET YOUR TODAY TO BE STOLEN by the ghost of YESTERDAY or the "To-Do" list of TOMORROW

Every mountain top is within reach if you just keep climbing

IT'S TIME to START LIVING THE LIFE YOU'VE IMAGINED

if you never never try} you'll never know

the voice of the SEA SPEAKS to the SOUL

A smooth sea never made a skilled sailor

WAKE UP AND BE AWESOME

the START is what STOPS
MOST PEOPLE

Try to be a RAINBOW ~in~ someone's cloud

"**SOME PEOPLE DREAM** of **SUCCESS,** OTHERS **STAY AWAKE** to **ACHIEVE IT.**"

WHEN TIMES ARE TOUGH DARE TO BE TOUGHER

> **PEOPLE OFTEN FORGET THAT KINDNESS IS FREE**

VINTAGE ST. PETE

and Vintage Pinellas

Volume 3

Published by St. Petersburg Press

St. Petersburg, FL

www.stpetersburgpress.com

@2023 St. Petersburg Press

All stories previously published in the St. Pete Catalyst 2022 and 2023

All rights reserved. No part of this publication may be reproduced, distributed, or transmitted in any form or by any means, including photocopying, recording or other electronic or mechanical methods, without the prior written permission of the publisher, except in the case of brief quotations embodied in critical reviews and certain other noncommercial uses permitted by copyright law. For permission requests contact St. Petersburg Press at www.stpetersburgpress.com.

Design and composition by St. Petersburg Press

Cover and interior design by Bill DeYoung and Isa Crosta

Hardcover ISBN: 978-1-940300-79-5

Paperback ISBN: 978-1-940300-80-1

First Edition

VINTAGE ST. PETE

and Vintage Pinellas

Volume 3

Bill DeYoung

@2023 St. Petersburg Press
All stories published in the *St. Pete Catalyst 2022 and 2023*

Table of Contents

Foreword 7

Restaurants 9

Smokin': Ted Peters' unlikely fish tale 11
The splendor of the Kapok Tree Inn 17
El Cap: 60 years of burgers and beers 27
The igloo on the beach: The Penguin 31
The lady and the Chattaway 39

Making History 43

Founding fathers and famous names 45
Center of activity: The Gulfport Casino 55
Curtain up! St. Petersburg Little Theatre 61
Parade Day: The Festival of States 69
The Beaux Arts Gallery and Coffeehouse 79
The Tarpon Springs sponge industry 87
The Pier, The Laser and Rockne Krebs 97
The US Coast Guard Blackthorn tragedy 103

Movies & TV 111

The WTVT Big 13 family album 113
Dick Crippen, swinging for the fences 127
Making a 'Strange' movie in Gulfport 135
Rolling: Still more movies on location 141
Warm Winters: The 'Dolphin Tale' movies 149

Larger than life 157

Takeoff: The legend of Albert Whitted 159
The man, the myth, the music: Lenny Dee 165
Hugh Boyd and HMS Bounty in Tahiti 175
Times keeper: Columnist Dick Bothwell 185
Fight for right: The Courageous Twelve 191
Stranger things: A rock 'n' roll saga 197
When we were kings: The Headlights 205

Acknowledgements 211
About the author 213

Foreword

Bill DeYoung is a master of the feature story, as you'll see in this third installment of *Vintage St. Pete*. His instinct for ferreting out the fascinating, yet often untold, stories of St. Petersburg's history is unerring. Lucky for us, he does the hard work of committing these stories to print; weaving together the facts, context, setting, and quotes that make a story sing.

Bill has a knack for asking the same questions I have as a reader, and goes about finding the answers, often in unusual places. His innate interest in his subject always shines through. He is a master interviewer, able to elicit, by turns, the most intimate emotions and the most uproarious of quotes. After reading *Vintage St. Pete 3*, I know I'll never be able to forget where Tom Reese told Jim Morrison to keep his junk.

Bill's stories remind us that the places that make our community special were not foregone conclusions. Ted Peters opened up his smoker when he heard a car coming, using the smoke to lure beachgoers to stop by. Lenny Dee drew people to his Dolphin Den with his humor and brilliance on the Hammond electric organ. These stories of local successes in business and entertainment remind us how the best rise to the top - through talent, yes, but more importantly through creativity and perseverance.

The stories offer an eminently readable synthesis of what any historian will recognize as hours of painstaking research. Bill includes the important facts that establish the story's credibility (who knew that a sponge is the exoskeleton of an animal?) while not skipping the anecdote that makes it a joy to read. Bill entertains while he educates.

Monica Kile
Historian and tour guide

RESTAURANTS

Although his restaurant's specialty was mullet, filleted and smoked over mangrove wood, Ted Peters himself was an avid fisherman who did not discriminate. In this 1960 photo he's showing off "lunker" sea trout he caught in Boca Ciega Bay. Lathrop family collection.

Early '50s, with few neighbors. That's Grandma Peters' 1951 Pontiac parked out front. Postcard image.

Smokin': Ted Peters' unlikely fish tale

Pasadena Avenue was just two narrow, patchwork lanes when Ted Peters bought a single acre of mangroves and sand in 1950. There were fruit stands but not much retail in the scrubby, salty wilderness, no professional buildings, no apartment complexes, no condo towers. The two gas stations on Pasadena had above-ground tanks.

You could cast a line right into the water across the road. Peters had to build a seawall, and backfill the rear of his property, to keep Boca Ciega Bay out. He hand-made the seawall out of palm trees, railroad ties and tar paper.

Ted Peters Famous Smoked Fish is still there, on the same land and in the same brown open-air wooden building Ted built with his half-brother and business partner Elry Lathrop, for their hard-earned and saved-up $15,000.

Mike Lathrop, Elry's son, now operates Ted Peters along with Jay Cook, Ted's grandson. During the busy season, they go through around 2,000 pounds of fish per week.

Lathrop has a theory about the restaurant's extraordinary staying power. "There's always been family members here that had an invested interest, no matter how hard they had to work or what they had to do, to make it run and run right," he said. "Most people don't have a lot of family that wants to continue in a restaurant, so they end up letting somebody manage it for them. And that's why it usually goes away."

Just like Ted and Elry, they've refused all

11

Peters made deliveries; before the restaurant, he regularly drove tubs of fish to the South Side of St. Petersburg. Lathrop family collection.

offers to sell the business – and, make no mistake, theirs is prime real estate. Has been since the '60s, when the population exploded.

Lathrop is proud that multiple generations of families know and love the place. "People just wanted to go back to something that always looked the same," he explained, "and always felt the same. And people keep saying to me: 'Don't mess this up. We want to come in here and see ugly green cafeteria plates.'

"Which, by the way, are very expensive."

Ted Peters was a master plumber in World War II-era Olean, N.Y. After his parents split, his mother married Elry's dad, and the extended, blended family made its way, over time, to St. Petersburg. Nobody missed the New York winters.

He was a dreamer, a hard worker and something of an opportunist, and he took a job at the Fisherman's Co-op on Madeira Beach.

"When Ted first got to Florida, to make money he went out to the beach, collecting fish from the co-op in a washtub with some ice," said Lathrop, who grew up in St. Petersburg. "And he would go down to the south side of St. Pete where people didn't have cars, and he'd go door to door selling fish."

One afternoon in 1946 he found an old, discarded fish smoker – a rough wooden box with sliding trays and space for a small bed of fire at the bottom – and dragged it home.

Soon he'd opened a restaurant – an old shack, really, with a hotplate and a couple of barstools inside – on Blind Pass Road. The Blue Anchor Inn's specialty was smoked mullet, a bony but tasty local fish that was readily available in local waters (by net – mullet don't generally bite on hooks). He fueled it with buttonwood mangrove branches.

"Everybody that smoked fish did it in their back yards, or in the woods," Lathrop said. "Nobody had ever put it up on the side of the road. That was Ted's claim to fame.

"He attached the old smoker to a telephone pole, which had a telephone booth on the other side of it. Whenever Ted would hear one of those old cars coming down the road – because they traveled so slow – he'd go out there and open the smoker up.

"And as it was smoking, the smoke would waft over and fill the phone booth with smoke. People would pull in and say 'Hey, your phone booth's on fire.'"

Inevitably, they'd leave with a belly full of mullet, and some of Grandma Peters' family recipe German potato salad. She started whipping it up, the family legend goes, because she'd grown tired of hand-cutting potatoes for French fries.

In late summer and fall, when business was slow, Ted and Elry became stone crabbers, and sold their catch to the local Mediterranean restaurants. Grandma and the boys' wives ran the restaurant in their absence.

In the smokehouse, 1965, with Ted, Grandma Peters and a smoked mullet ready for the plate. Tampa Bay Times/Zuma Press.

South Pasadena, in 1951 when Ted Peters and Elry Lathrop moved in, was an unincorporated part of Pinellas County known as Coreytown. Most of the businesses on the trail were after-hours bottle clubs; Coreytown was rough and it was lawless – the police did not patrol there.

Coreytown was abolished when local property owners – spurred on by Ted and Elry – pushed to incorporate the area as South Pasadena (they needed a minimum of 25 registered voters to do so). With this came blue laws – no drinking allowed after midnight – and the end of the bottle clubs.

Ted Peters was looking ahead. St. Petersburg Beach was being developed at a rapid clip. As the main thoroughfare to the beach, Pasadena Avenue would soon be clogged with traffic. And that meant customers for his smoked mullet and king mackerel, his secret-recipe fish spread and his mom's potato salad and fruit pies.

He built a bigger smokehouse – without an attached phone booth – to catch folks by the nose.

Although they'd both served in the Armed Forces during the war, it was Elry who went to college (on the GI bill). He'd take the summer off and run the restaurant while Ted stretched his legs. They had a one-month-on, one-month-off arrangement that lasted pretty much until Elry's death in 1990.

His dad and his uncle, Lathrop recalled, had built a special life for themselves and their families.

"They came to Florida to enjoy Florida. And they loved Florida. They liked to play golf, they liked to scallop, they liked to oyster. They loved to fish. They loved just being on the water. These guys were all about fun – that's why they didn't want to own multiple restaurants."

"No self-respecting kid didn't know how to sharpen a stick and snatch a mullet," Mike Lathrop says. "You could always sell 'em, you could always smoke 'em." St. Pete Catalyst.

They worked just enough to keep the business successful, and earn a comfortable living. Ted bought and sold property, and he and Elry invested in Englewood, a rustic fishing village in Sarasota County.

He was married to Elena, his New York sweetheart, for nearly 60 years. She passed in 1993.

Although Peters eventually retired from the day-to-day restaurant business, he stopped by every morning. Sitting at a corner barstool, nursing a cup of coffee, he'd glad-hand the customers, telling stories about the old days, and give the waitresses a good-natured hard time.

"How long has Ted Peters been dead?"

The waitress called Surly Shirley leans across the counter, scowls and points left.

"He's sitting next to you."

From his well-worn stool, silver-haired Ted Peters beams with pleasure. He has big white teeth and eyes blue as the back of a tuna. He's small, wiry and wizened like a man who has spent many decades toiling in a smokehouse - which he has.

Jeff Klinkenberg/St. Petersburg Times Dec. 15, 1999

Well into his ninth decade, Ted was full of energy. He loved to dance – he had a (younger) girlfriend – and was a frequent visitor to the Oasis Pub on Corey Avenue, where he'd bellow along tunelessly to the oldies performed by the house band.

In February, 2001, he was darting across Gulfport Boulevard, around the corner from the institution that still bears his name, when he was struck by an automobile driven by a 94-year-old woman. He died three days later. He was 91.

There have been changes. Mangrove was outlawed as a fuel source more than 50 years ago; the restaurant uses red oak exclusively. Until the use of purse seines and gill nets was abolished in the '90s, area mullet populations dwindled. Now, the fish are taken almost exclusively with cast nets – and, according to Mike Lathrop, they've come back strong.

Ted Peters Famous Smoked Fish buys its mullet and Spanish mackerel exclusively from Gulf Coast fishermen. Mahi mahi is sourced from Florida. Salmon, which Mike

Ted at the bar, 1999. "He has big white teeth and eyes blue as the back of a tuna," Jeff Klinkenberg wrote. Tampa Bay Times/Zuma Press.

Lathrop added to the menu a number of years ago, is imported. These days, "It's our biggest seller. By a bunch."

The restaurant is still on a cash-only basis, but that will probably be changing at some point. The future never sleeps.

What won't change, Lathrop is sure, is the "family-operated" nature of the business.

Richard Carroll is general manager. "Richard's married to Ted's great-granddaughter," he said. "So his children are Ted Peters' great-great grandchildren. And who knows, they may get shanghaied into working at the restaurant, too. Richard and I are talking about it already.

"That's how it happens here. I got shanghaied into this. I was supposed to work for two weeks."

The Florida Room, one of 12 separate dining areas at the Kapok Tree Inn. Unless indicated, all photos in this story are postcard images.

Robert Hoyt's tree is still there, healthy and thriving and standing around 120 feet tall; the leafy branches reach out high over today's McMullen-Booth Road. St. Pete Catalyst.

The splendor of the Kapok Tree Inn

It all began with a little tree, a sapling brought from its native India in the 1880s by orange grove owner Robert D. Hoyt, and planted in his front yard in unincorporated southeastern Clearwater, near the edge of Tampa Bay in an area known as Cooper's Point.

Called Java Cotton, Bombax or by its genus, Ceiba, the most common name for the fast-growing soft-wood tree with bright red flowers is Kapok. The Kapok tree.

Robert Hoyt's tree is still there, healthy and thriving and standing around 120 feet tall. Its gnarled trunk has a 20-foot circumference. The leafy branches reach out high over today's McMullen-Booth Road.

For 33 years, this tree stood sentinel at the entrance to the most popular, and financially successful, restaurant on the Gulf coast of Florida, and possibly the entire state. During its golden era, the 1960s and '70s, the Kapok Tree Inn served up to 1,700 guests per day.

They came to be seated in one of 12 dining rooms, each lavishly decorated with Greek and Roman statuary, ornate chandeliers and other European furniture, fixtures, tiles, paintings and ephemera, some of it faux, some very old and very real and shipped to the Kapok Tree Inn from Europe. Frescos, carvings and paneling flourishes were carefully replicated. Chiseled moldings were purchased from vintage theaters in New York. There were plants everywhere.

Each room was different. Your party might be seated in the Gallery Room, the Chandelier Room, the Florida Room, the Red Room, the Grape Room or the Zebra Lounge.

The two main buildings were connected by an extensive Mediterranean garden, with more statues, topiary and elaborate Renaissance-inspired fountains.

The architect of Clearwater's Disneyland of dining was Richard Baumgardner, a Maryland saxophone player, singer and bandleader who'd cut a number of 78 RPM dance records under the name Dick "Hot Cha" Gardner. Hot Cha's mother had turned the family home, in the town of Urbana, into a "homestyle" restaurant called the Peter Pan Inn.

After his music career ended, Baumgardner returned home and added the Hot Cha Supper Club, and when his mother died in 1945, he overhauled the entire establishment, putting in roomfuls of antiques and kitsch, creating a unique dining experience for families looking for a weekend meal and something interesting to do. The Peter Pan, with its five distinct dining rooms, was by design a "destination."

Clearwater was a favorite winter vacation spot for Baumgardner, his wife Ethel and their three kids. At some point in the '50s he bought the grove once owned by Robert Hoyt and began to plan a bigger restaurant, custom-crafted, with an unusual and alluring atmosphere. The family became Floridians.

The giant flowering tree out front was already something of a tourist draw. So Baumgardner named his venture the Kapok Tree Inn.

It was a hit right out of the gate. The menu was not elaborate – for years, the entrees were just ham, fried chicken, fried shrimp or T-bone steak, all served with

roasted potatoes, hush-puppies, green peas and a "Lazy Susan" relish tray.

The simplicity of the offerings was not the point. Tickets for the meal of choice were purchased from a gilded booth at the entrance, inside the 300-foot, high-ceilinged "mall," and before proceeding to their assigned dining room, visitors were encouraged to traverse the winding garden paths, like the hedge and fountain mazes on the backside of an ostentatious European palace. Painters, glass blowers and other artisans worked continuously in the gardens, adding to the ambiance.

Benefit luncheons with fashion shows are popularly found at The Inn, and last week a group of Tampa bankers were spotted meeting there for Innish treats ... give a man one of these, and he'll be nigh too happy to notice the glamor of his surroundings.

Tampa Tribune/Sept. 20, 1961

In May 1964, Ethel Baumgardner, who was in the process of divorcing her husband, died suddenly at age 50. Less than two months later, Richard Baumgardner married Kapok Tree waitress June Eader, 22 years his junior.

In 1968, the couple opened Baumgardner's, a formal, coat-and-tie restaurant, across McMullen-Booth Road (then

known as Florida State Road 593) from the Kapok Tree Inn.

Business was booming. The company went public in 1970 and opened other Kapok Tree restaurants in Madeira Beach, Fort Lauderdale and Daytona Beach. By mid-decade, the Kapok Tree Inn Corporation was reporting net profits of around $1 million annually.

Richard Baumgarder died in 1976, the same year the Kapok Tree Inn was named one of the top 100 restaurants in United States by *Sales and Marketing Management* magazine. June donated 38 acres of land to the City of Clearwater with the provision that it be used for a performing arts venue, to be known as the Richard B. Baumgardner Center. Drugstore magnate Jack Eckerd bought naming rights for the facility, and used it to honor his wife, Ruth.

As the result of an ugly, protracted court battle between his widow and Baumgarder's children, her majority shares were sold in 1984 to Houston businessman Murray Steinfeld.

The new owner brought in Aaron Fodiman as a partner and manager of the restaurant. Among the many changes, Fodiman upgraded the menu, and the service, and eliminated the outdated "ticket" system for ordering meals.

Baumgarder's, the fine dining place across McMullen-Booth, became the Savoy Dinner Club. A series of gift shops were installed inside the greenhouse-like mall, just behind the titular tree.

And business picked up.

But Steinfeld – whose endgame was to make money from the restaurant, and in time sell the real estate for enormous profit – died in 1988. And he left storm clouds roiling.

"Everything went exactly as it was supposed to," recalls Fodiman, "except for the fact that Steinfeld was heavily involved in real estate in Texas, and he borrowed $5 million against the property from an insurance company. And when he was unable to repay the $5 million, they took the property."

The Kapok Tree restaurants in Madeira Beach and the other Florida cities were closed and sold off. Even the sale (for $2 million) of the Savoy Dinner Club to the state, so it could be demolished for the widening of McMullen-Booth, couldn't stem the Chapter 11 tide.

The irony, says Fodiman, who's editor and publisher of *Tampa Bay* magazine, was that the Kapok Tree Inn was operating at a profit when he was forced to close it – without any advance warning to the 300 employees, many of whom showed up for work to find the doors locked, on May 14, 1991.

Indeed, *Restaurants and Institutions* magazine reported, in March – just two months before the restaurant closed – that Kapok Tree business was up 12 percent in 1990.

"For me," Fodiman explains, "it will always be my love. It was an incredible place, we did unbelievable things there, we put on great fundraisers for the community. It was a very special place."

The following year, Kentucky Central Life Insurance Co. sold the business and land to 38-year-old Elliott Rubinson, owner of Thoroughbred Music stores in Tampa and Sarasota, for $1.3 million.

"When I saw the foreclosure sale and I saw the low bids, I figured, I've got to get in here and make some kind of offer," Rubinson told the *St. Petersburg Times*. "This is a once-in-a-lifetime opportunity."

After deciding they didn't want to be in

Jasmen Marley's father was a dishwasher at the Kapok Tree Inn as a teenager. Today, she is Director of Sales & Events for Kapok Special Events. St. Pete Catalyst.

the restaurant business, Rubinson and his wife Pam turned the main building – the mall – into a Thoroughbred store. They leased the facility to national music retailer Sam Ash in 1999.

The Sam Ash store is still there today. It is, doubtless, the most curiously decorated guitar-and-keyboard outlet in the world, as many of Hot Cha's statues, arches and faux marble columns have been left in place.

Elliott Rubinson passed away in 2017. Pam runs Kapok Special Events out of the second building, between the immaculately-manicured Renaissance gardens, where water still flows from the ornate fountains of the Baumgardner and Fodiman eras.

Similarly, the dining rooms are kept brilliant and sparkling, the imported chandeliers swaying from white ceilings, with polished mahogany pieces and exotic light fixtures in each room.

The calendar is packed with weddings, proms, parties and other social gatherings; there's no kitchen, however.

For some, it's a time warp, a happy reminder of an era long gone.

According to Events Director Jasmen Marley, an equal amount of visitors have never heard of the famous Kapok Tree Inn.

"Some people come in from out of town, and they remember it," she explains. "I don't want this place to die in the memory of just the previous visitors. I want everybody to know that this place is alive, it's still thriving. It's a little hidden gem in Clearwater that a lot of people just don't know about."

stpete
AUG+SEP 10 VOL 1 ED 2
MAGAZINE

Mary Jean Bonfili on the cover of St. Pete Magazine, 2010.

El Cap regulars, sometime in the '70s. This photo is in a frame on the restaurant wall.

El Cap: 60 years of burgers and beers

hen Pennsylvania transplants Steve and Rose Bonfili bought a tiny 4th Street tavern called El Cap in 1963, and transformed it into a stop-n-go sandwich shop, they were taking a risk – albeit a calculated one.

Recently widened, 4th was the most-traveled commercial thoroughfare in St. Petersburg at the time, and the El Cap was located midway between the city's two biggest tourist attractions, Sunken Gardens and the Florida Wildlife Ranch, a stone's throw in either direction.

Nearing 65 years old since the place first opened, El Cap has been renovated and expanded, yet it's one of just a handful of St. Pete restaurants seemingly untouched by time. Although stacked ham sandwiches were the top menu item in the early '60s, El Cap made its reputation on hamburgers, made fresh and one-by-one, with cold beer and neighborly camaraderie on the side.

Bartender Larry Chopard has worked at El Cap for nearly 30 years, as has patty-maker Johnny Johnson. Co-owner Cynthia Nally, who started as a server, has been there almost as long.

She and Tara Mattiacci – until recently, another co-owner - were hired by Frank Bonfili, Steve and Rose's son, who took over management in the early 1980s. Over time, Frank and his wife Mary Jean expanded the physical space by buying nextdoor properties, and transformed El Cap into a sports bar, perhaps the first such establishment in St. Pete.

He was front of house; she managed the kitchen.

Frank, a baseball nut, covered the walls with pennants, photos and other memorabilia, and installed several TVs for at-the-bar game watching. Every item on the El Cap menu was given catchy sports-centric names.

Frank Bonfili was the kind of guy, they say, who greeted every customer personally as they walked in the door. He was outgoing and gregarious, and argued louder than anyone that Tampa Bay should have its own MLB team.

He bought season tickets for the Tampa Bay Devil Rays' inaugural year, which was to begin in the spring of 1998. He and Mary Jean agreed to start opening El Cap on Sundays, because – he pronounced – with 81 home games, there were going to be a lot of hungry people in town.

Frank Bonfili died of a heart attack on March 13, 1997. He was 46.

A bit of history. The little building at 3500 4th Street North originated in 1948; it was, most likely, a pub some believe was called Bruno's (records from this time are difficult to find). In 1958, one Louis Joseph Svabek bought the property and re-named the business El Cap. Svabek registered three other St. Pete pubs - Nite Cap, Sun Cap and Old Cap – and one in Largo, Hub Cap.

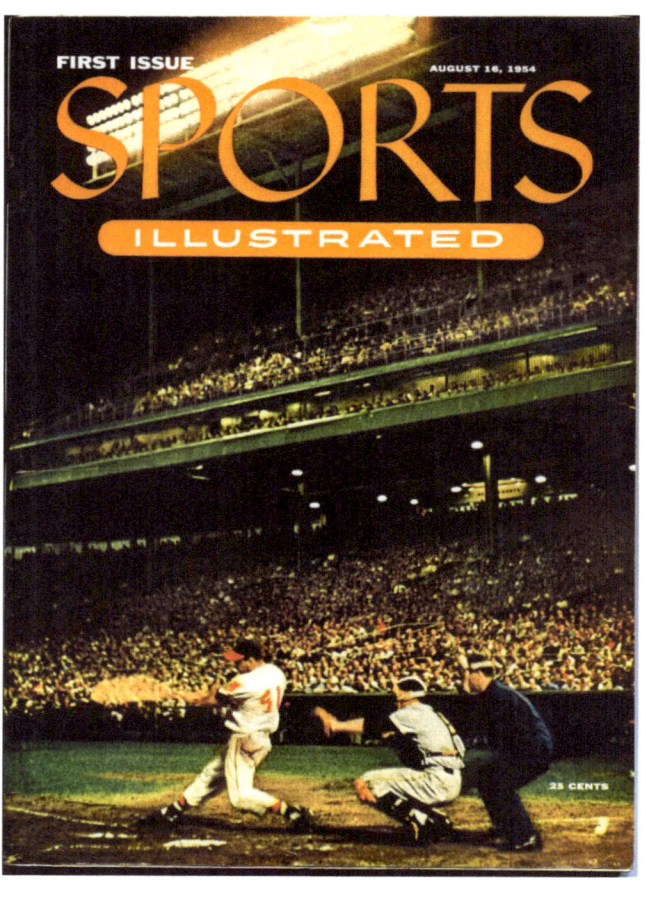

And in 1963, he sold El Cap to Frank Bonfili's parents. The senior Bonfili's half-brother was New York-based National League umpire Augie Donatelli, who visited St. Petersburg every year for Spring Training. He encouraged Steve and his wife to invest in the city, "a nice place where a lot of baseball people go."

Donatelli, who appeared in an action photo on the cover of the first issue of Sports Illustrated in 1954, retired to St. Petersburg in 1973, and sometimes held court from the bar at El Cap.

Following Frank's passing, Mary Jean became the central figure in the El Cap story.

Frank Bonfili, baseball fan, behind the bar, 1990. Bonfili family collection.

"She was fun to work with," says Tara Mattiacci. "And she was a people person, so she really enjoyed being behind the bar and talking to her customers. Everybody knew her."

Mattiacci's parents had been friendly with Frank and Mary Jean; they were all part of a group of couples who enjoyed evenings out together at Derby Lane. "I was kind of raised around El Cap," Mattiacci explains.

Looking for a job in 2001, Mattiacci asked her family friend if there were any openings at El Cap. She was handed an order pad and shown the menu on the wall.

Cindy Nally signed on soon afterwards. They were hired as waitresses, but "we trained to do everything. That's the way Mary Jean was back then." Soon, Mattiacci and Nally were co-managers.

Around 2016 the widowed Mary Jean – who had no children - told them she'd changed her will. She intended to leave El Cap to them, her loyal management team. "She said that she wanted us to keep it the way it was," relayed Mattiacci.

May Jean Bonfili, 66, died of cancer May 28, 2019.

Mattiacci retired at the tail end of 2022, selling her half of El Cap to the investment group Seed & Feed Hospitality.

Cindy Nally stayed on as half-owner and fulltime manager, and she still greets customers as they come in the door. "I love El Cap, and I'm really excited about these guys coming aboard," Nally explained. "And I think it'll be a wonderful thing for us, and for the community as well. Keep this little corner cozy and friendly and welcoming."

The former Penguin Restaurant site, at 8000 Gulf Boulevard, Treasure Island. The Treasure Island Beach Pavilion was dedicated in 2013. The city paid $1,325,000 for the beachfront property in 1999. St. Pete Catalyst.

The Penguin Restaurant in the mid '70s, letting a tropical storm roll right over - and under. Jackie Greene/Tampa Bay Times/Zuma Press

The igloo on the beach: The Penguin

he most unusual building in Pinellas County met the wrecking ball in 1999, but the title remains unchallenged to this day.

At 8000 Gulf Boulevard, Treasure Island – near the southern tip of the area known as Sunset Beach – the Penguin Restaurant was a tri-humped marvel of modern architecture, a 250-foot-long dome made of high-tensile concrete sprayed over steel rebar ribs. Its 7,000 contiguous square feet stood atop pilings 16 feet off the sand, 29 large porthole windows offering diners unparalleled views of shore and sunset.

The Penguin was a smooth-sided, snow-white concrete igloo, designed with curves, without corners or seams, so that hurricane winds would have nothing to latch onto and tear apart.

Seating 260, the Penguin's specialty was prime rib of beef, which owner/chef Winston Hunter sliced tableside from a little motorized cart. Hunter's Yorkshire pudding was also well-known. Seafood, of course, was always on the menu.

Yet the food, and the full bar, were almost secondary. When you went to the Penguin, you went to that weird-looking place out at the beach. You parked underneath the kitchen – by necessity the largest part of the dome – and walked up the long ramp into something else altogether.

It was all done by design. In 1972, Hurricane Agnes had destroyed the old wooden Penguin Restaurant. In the restaurant's three-decade history, storms had damaged or totaled it numerous times.

Architect Ronn Ginn, 89, remembers the day Hunter told him he had the guarantee of a $300,000 loan from the Small Business Association's Disaster Relief Fund, with a 1 percent interest rate, provided he could make the "new" Penguin virtually hurricane-proof.

Says Ginn, who's still a working architect: "It was not designed to quote-unquote be different. It was designed to meet the requirements we were given by the SBA." And guidelines set down by the Federal Disaster Assistance Administration, under the auspices of the Department of Housing and Urban Development, which would evolve into the independent Federal Emergency Management Agency (FEMA) in 1979.

Hunter, Ginn, recalls, "was a great client. He said 'Ron, it's your job. I'm a chef. I've been a chef all my life, and people love my food. I'm gonna stick to what I know.'"

And Ronn Ginn loved a challenge.

Under construction at Sunset Beach, the Penguin club, newest private club at the beaches, will have a large social room with an open fireplace, a dining room with many windows overlooking the water, a long front porch and a large bathhouse. The clubroom will be flanked by two wings containing the dining room and bathhouse. M. Winfield Lott is the architect.

In the 1930s, every beach community in Pinellas County had its own private club, where the reasonably well-to-do could swim, engage in light water and sand sports, dine, drink, dance and play cards; they were also leased out, on occasion, for public civic and club meetings. The Penguin Club opened in August 1939.

"The main building of the club consists of a spacious lounge room and dining room separated by a semi-circular bar and a great fireplace," gushed the *St. Petersburg Times* in its "Over the Causeways" section. "Knotty pine paneling with rustic cypress trim and an inverted ceiling add coziness to the lounge room, while the dining room is finished with mahogany stain walls and trimmed in rich walnut."

The "well-planned bathhouse," the story said, "has accommodations for 100 guests." Searchlights were aimed at the beach for after-dark swimming.

"Theme" nights were popular – the newspaper duly reported every guest at the Penguin's "Wild West Night," bridge, volleyball and badminton contests ("Prizes of Old Spice perfume were given the winners"), a Mexican-themed wedding and more. Members frequently went bowling together.

The founders were Hubert McNally and Arthur Barnes, proud members of the St. Petersburg Jaycees. McNally and his wife Elizabeth had an infant son, Terrence, born the previous November at St. Anthony's Hospital.

Terrence McNally would grow up to become the Tony-winning playwright of *Kiss of the Spider Woman, Ragtime, Master Class, Love! Valour! Compassion!* and others. The *New York Times* called McNally "The Bard of American Theater."

His parents sold the Penguin Club in 1941, and moved with tiny Terrence to Port Chester, N.Y.

A hurricane severely damaged the Penguin Club in June, 1944, destroying a seawall and other barriers, and a fire two months later sealed the deal, necessitating a near-total rebuild.

Five years on, then-new owners Stephen and Clara Girard rebuilt the old place again – elevating it off the sand via short wooden pilings – after a Labor Day blow all but obliterated it for a second time.

The Girards declared the Penguin a restaurant open to the public – a private club no more – in 1952.

Clara Girard sold the Penguin in 1959 before departing for a lengthy European visit; by '63, however, she was back, in full ownership mode again, and had hired Winston Hunter as head chef. Hunter's specialty was prime rib of beef with Yorkshire pudding.

The 1960s brought more harsh tropical weather, and another damaging fire, and by decade's end Hunter had convinced Girard to sell the battered restaurant to him.

Things were going just swell until Hurricane Agnes arrived, near the end of June in 1972. Hunter estimated the damage at around $100,000 – the entire floor had fallen through, followed by the roof – and he boldly told the *Times* "We're coming back. We're not discouraged."

How he was going to pull it off, he had no idea. So he went looking for an architect, and he found Ronn Ginn.

According to the land survey, Hunter owned everything from the road to the water. The first step was putting up the new place closer to Gulf Boulevard, farther away from the pummeling surf.

Battered at the back door. The "old" Penguin in 1964. George Trabant/St. Petersburg Times/Zuma Press.

Away from the naive footprint set down in 1939.

The SBA insisted Ginn's design had to withstand winds up to 150 miles per hour, stand well above any possible tide surge, and be wheelchair accessible.

Ginn had recently been contacted by a South Florida engineer who'd created a new, hyper-strong form of concrete, and used it to great effect in the hurricane-battered Caribbean. Mixing cement with a chemical additive produced a compound that could withstand 12,000 pounds of pressure per square inch, four times the norm for structural concrete in 1972.

The wet concrete could be sprayed pneumatically, with high pressure, over a ribcage of steel rebar, producing a virtually impenetrable eggshell finish.

Ginn had his builder drive 55 steel pilings, filled with concrete, as much as 85 feet into the ground. The restaurant's floor, when all was said and done, stood 16 feet off the Sunset Beach sand.

At the top – 60 feet in the air – the concrete shell was 3 and ½ inches thick. It was eight inches at its base, where the floor was welded to the pilings.

There were no stairs to carry patrons up to the restaurant from the ground-level parking. Instead, Ginn designed a massive, dogleg ramp up the side of the building, which fulfilled the SBA requirement. Hunter felt this was more aesthetically pleasing than stairs, for those who could manage it (although he did install a discreet elevator).

Inside, says Ginn, Hunter wanted it all open, from one end to the other with no columns, the better to ride his cart between the kitchen (the only room, aside from the restrooms, with a dividing wall), the bar and the dining area.

It was all part of the Penguin experience.

Some visitors have thought the vast white caves of the interior seemed too barren while others, myself included, felt comfortable in the organic vaulted space, albeit, return to the womb and all that psychological stuff ... a flat plastered ceiling could have been dropped from the curve to accommodate the lighting and air conditioning ductwork which runs between the shells, but Ginn opted, I think correctly, to continue the curvature.

Charles Benbow, St. Petersburg Times/July 10, 1974

35

It may not have been pretty, but it was pretty distinctive.

"They flew a reporter and photographer down from the *Boston Herald*," Ginn remembers. "They didn't believe this building was going to withstand anything. They thought I was a blowhard, just another blowhard architect."

Architects, he laughs, "don't blow hard." The rules and regulations they follow are strict and to-the-point.

Only Mother Nature, it seemed, was blowing hard. Never, in the quarter-century it occupied the real estate at 8000 Gulf Boulevard did the Ginn Penguin shudder or shake from the pounding of hurricane wind or water.

Due to illness, Hunter sold the Penguin in 1980, and over the following decade it changed hands, and names, several times. It became Bedrox, a gay and lesbian dance club, in 1989 (so named because the owners thought the building resembled something out of *The Flintstones*). They painted the futuristic façade pink.

Bedrox rolled along for a while, attracting the enthusiasm of large crowds – and

irritation from its Sunset Beach neighbors, who regularly complained about drunkenness and brawling, nudity and even sex on the beach after dark.

The club's owners filed for bankruptcy in 1997, and a sale to the City of Treasure Island was proffered.

Using Penny For Pinellas tax money, the city paid Kim Costanza $1,325,000 for the building and the acre-plus of prime beachfront property. "It really has to be open to the public," a consulting architect told the *Tampa Tribune*. "However long it takes to accomplish that remains to be seen. It's just a shell."

The Bedrox years.

Postcard image.

"I hate to see the building itself go," Treasure Island mayor Leon Atkinson said. "Because it's such an icon."

Nevertheless, it was decided to raze Bedrox and construct a public access pavilion on the site, with a gazebo, playground, restrooms and re-planted beds of sand-protecting sea oats.

On July 26, 1999, the city's designated demolition contractor aimed a 5,300-pound solid steel wrecking ball at the erstwhile Penguin. "They didn't really explain to him how strong it was," Ronn Ginn recalls gleefully, "because they didn't know. But that building had been there for almost 50 years. He didn't understand that the concrete we poured in there got stronger with age.

"Here comes this big ol' crane with a huge wrecking ball. Usually, you hit something like that, and it's gone.

"But that big wrecking ball, instead of going through the dome, it bounced off."

Eventually, of course, the curve was crushed and the building demolished. The Treasure Island Beach Pavilion was dedicated in 2013.

A Briton by birth, Jillian Frers turned an old game room into the Chattaway's English tea room. St. Pete Catalyst.

City of St. Petersburg.

The lady and the Chattaway

Should any member of England's royal family ever make a quick whistlestop in St. Petersburg, odds are the itinerary would include afternoon tea at the Chattaway. One of the city's longest-lived restaurants, it's the only place in town to combine funky Floridian roadside charm with centuries-old British tradition.

Should a Royal or two feel like a burger and a side of slaw, the Chattaway will have them covered, too.

The afternoon teas were the brainchild of Jillian Frers, who's owned the restaurant – at the intersection of 4th Street and 22nd Avenue South – since the mid 1970s. If arrangements are made in advance, she'll serve up the English tea, with scones, petit fours and wee little finger sandwiches, in the semi-formal dining room.

A Londoner by birth, Frers had followed her first husband to St. Pete and a new start. After that marriage ended, and the one after that, she found herself a divorced mother of six without a lot of options.

As a hobby, she began to perform in plays at the St. Petersburg and Clearwater Little Theaters, and that's where she met Everett Lund, a well-regarded local actor and singer; they appeared together in *The Odd Couple*.

"He was my best friend," says Frers, 86. "He gets a crush on me, and he's going to take care of me. I'm with six kids and the ex-husband's not giving me any money. So life becomes difficult."

Lund proposed, and soon Jillian was

part-owner of the Chattaway, which Everett's mother had purchased in 1951.

Constructed in the early '20s, the building housed a general store for its first decade – it included a bar and a handful of rough-hewn stools – before being converted into a sandwich-and-beer joint in the wake of Prohibition. By the time ambitious New York divorcee Helen Lund bought the place, it was already called the Chattaway. Everett's mom always said she never found out what the name was supposed to mean, if anything.

Then, as now, the main draw of the Chattaway was its outdoor dining area, shady and comfortable, ribbed with picnic table and painted benches, planted with flowers and gaily decorated. There are 44 bathtubs ringing the property, each brightly painted and planted from the drain up with flowers. The place has character to spare.

It was always a family business. All of Jillian's kids did turns at the Chattaway; Everett was a waiter.

A waiter with a reputation. "It's a very famous, very well-known and very true story," Frers reports.

Everett was mouthy. He was brusque. He could be rude. Customers used to drop by just to get insulted by the big man in the apron; for the most part, they couldn't tell if he was kidding or not. He was a gifted storyteller, and even his tirades were entertaining.

To everyone except Jillian's kids, to whom he was incessantly vicious. "And you never knew when, or why," explains Frers' daughter, Amanda Kitto, the Chattaway's manager. "It was never provoked. It was just your turn. He could do it to us, or to Mom. Well, not so much to Mom. He was sometimes so wonderful, and sometimes such a jerk."

Still, he worked hard, especially after Helen's death. Everett would come in early, usually before dawn, and stay until closing.

The Chattaway opened in 1951. The building dated from 1922 – it was originally Four Corners Grocery. Ken Breslauer collection.

Family affair: Leah Poe, left, her mother Amanda Kitto (Chattaway manager), Chad Pearson (Leah's boyfriend) and matriarch Jillian Frers. St. Pete Catalyst.

In 1981, after 30 years of leasing the land under their building, he and Jillian bought the site, free and clear.

They were married for 17 increasingly fractious years. "If you insult one more customer," she eventually told him, "I'm leaving you." He did, and she did. "I divorced him for being a pri--," she smiles. But they remained friends even after the divorce, and continued to run the Chattaway together.

Jillian married Warren Frers, one of Everett's closest friends since their boyhood days in New York. "I married his best friend – and he still loved me," she says. "And he still loved his best friend." Warren Frers worked as the Chattaway's host, although he did not have a financial stake in the restaurant.

It was 1999 – three years before Everett's death – that Jillian began converting the restaurant's dingy game room into an "English tea room," with appropriate furniture, china, silver and decorations. "We did it slowly – we'd buy one table at a time, and chairs to match," she says. She began calling herself Lady Chattaway, for no other reason that it sounded very British.

Everett Lund left the Chattaway to his ex-wife in his will. Warren Frers passed away in 2010.

Today, it's still a family business. Says manager Kitto: "I always tell people, none of us drives a Mercedes; we're just here doing what we do, and nobody's wealthy over it. But we love it."

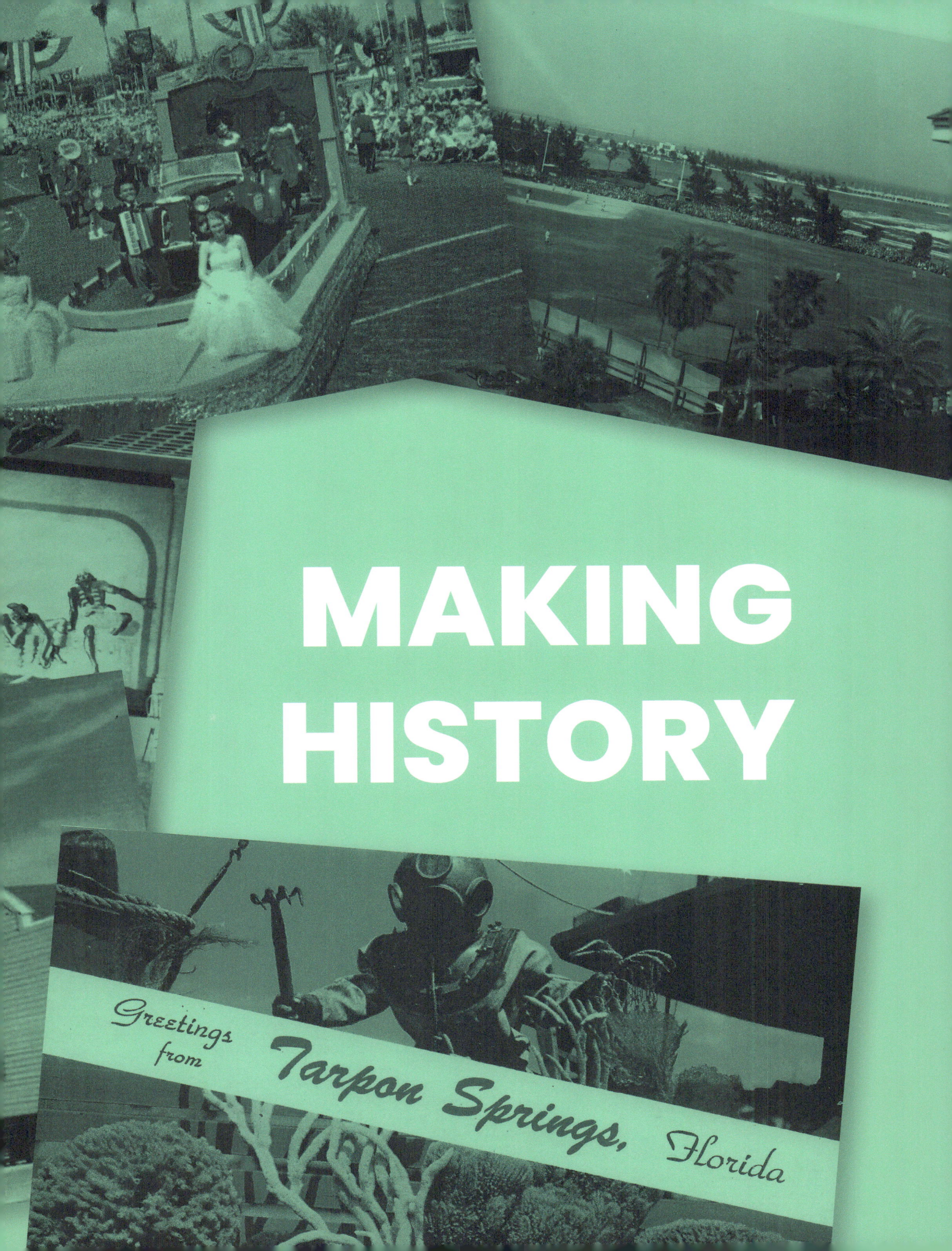

MAKING HISTORY

Sculptor John D. Hair's statue of Elder Jordan, adjacent to the Manhattan Casino, was dedicated in 2020. St. Pete Catalyst.

The scenic Roser Park neighborhood was named for its builder, Charles Roser. City of St. Petersburg.

Founding fathers and famous names

hat's in a name?" William Shakespeare wrote in *Romeo and Juliet*, adding: "That which we call a rose by any other name would smell just as sweet."

To expound, if St. Petersburg had been given the name Detroit, as was suggested by one of the city's pioneers, would it still be the St. Petersburg we know and love?

The city was founded in 1888, and incorporated four years later, and many of the names so familiar to residents today were attached to real people, the majority of whom played important roles in the first half-century (and more) of local history.

These are names you'll see as you cross a bridge, or walk through a park, stroll a neighborhood or ponder a monument. They all existed, and they all made marks on St. Pete so significant that those who came afterwards believed they should always be somewhere close by, if only in name and in memory.

Demens Landing Park is named for **Peter Demens**, one of the most important individuals in the city's early history and evolution. Born Pyotr Dementyev in 1849 into a wealthy family in Tver Oblast, Russia, he served in the Tzar's military, and was in fact the sentry commander at the royal family's Winter Palace. Exiled because of his political leanings in 1881, he arrived in Florida (he had a cousin living in Jacksonville) with $3,000, and changed his name to the American-sounding Peter Demens. Within four years he was operating a successful lumber business, and

Demens Landing Park was named for pioneer Peter Demens (insert), who also gave St. Petersburg its name. City of St. Petersburg photos.

bought into the burgeoning Orange Belt Railway. Demens brought the end of the rail line to rural, western Hillsborough (now Pinellas) County; the settlement had no official name. According to legend, Demens and prominent landowner John C. Williams reportedly flipped a coin to decide who would name the new city. Williams would have called it Detroit, after his hometown, but Demens won the toss and the place became St. Petersburg – after the Russian City in which young Pyotr had spent his childhood. According to St. Petersburg Museum of History Director Rui Farias, however, the real story is far less colorful: Demens announced, publicly, that the terminus of the railroad would be "in St. Petersburg," and Williams, who needed the Orange Belt business, simply let the persuasive Russian have his way.

Founded as Florida Presbyterian College in 1958, the school was re-named Eckerd College 14 years later, after drugstore magnate **Jack Eckerd** donated $12.5 million. Eckerd later tried, and failed, to get elected to the Florida Legislature, and to the governor's office. Today, the 1,500-store-strong Eckerd Drugs chain is long gone, and Jack is remembered mostly for his philanthropy. Although the land for Clearwater's premiere performing arts venue was donated to the city by the founders of the nearby Kapok Tree Inn, the venue was ultimately named for Jack Eckerd's wife and fellow philanthropist, Ruth.

The Courtney Campbell Causeway, crossing Old (northern) Tampa Bay and connecting Tampa and Clearwater, bears the name of **Courtney W.**

Campbell, a member of the Florida State Road Board (now known as the Department of Transportation) in the 1940s. Campbell's activism on behalf of the dilapidated Davis Causeway – named for construction boss Ben T. Davis, who owned it – was a major factor in getting the convenient over-water thoroughfare purchased by the state, repaired, beautified and brought up to speed. Thus, it was re-named in his honor (in 1948). Campbell was a resident of Clearwater Beach and served one term in the U.S. House, representing Florida's 1st congressional district.

Gandy Bridge (and Tampa's Gandy Boulevard) are named for **George "Dad" Gandy.** A financier, businessman and practical engineer obsessed with

John Williams (insert) and Williams Park today. St. Pete Catalyst.

Jonathan Gibbs. St. Petersburg Museum of History.

transportation and its endless possibilities, Gandy came to St. Petersburg from Philadelphia in 1903 to build and operate the city's trolley system. In 1915, Gandy set his considerable sights on constructing a traffic bridge over Tampa Bay. It took a while to raise capital for the privately-owned crossing, but Gandy in 1922 began selling stock in the project (cost: $1.9 million), and the three-mile Gandy Bridge – at the time the longest over-water bridge in the world – was dedicated by the governor of Florida in 1924. Gandy Bridge, now owned by the state, was redesigned and rebuilt several times over the ensuing decades.

The Howard Frankland (never "Franklin") Bridge is named in honor of Tampa banker and transportation advocate

W. Howard Frankland. He was a member of the State Road Board when he worked to devise plans for a fourth Tampa Bay crossing to ease traffic loads on nearby Gandy Bridge, and – perhaps more pressing – to become the next link in Florida's part of the federal Interstate highway system (for this reason, the U.S. government paid for 90 percent of the bridge's $16 million cost). Since re-designed and altered several times (new construction is going on even as you're reading this), the Howard Frankland Bridge opened Jan. 16, 1960. And right out of the gate there were gripes that it would not help much: "Traffic experts have predicted the mid-bay bridge will be dumping 75,000 cars a day into Pinellas in five years, most of it being funneled into St. Petersburg," the *Times* newspaper wrote on opening day, "which has only 4th and 9th Streets to handle the flow right now."

Dixie Hollins. St. Petersburg Museum of History.

St. Petersburg's Gibbs High School takes its name from **Jonathan C. Gibbs**, Florida's first Black Secretary of State (1868-72) and Superintendent of Public Instruction (1873-74). During the country's Reconstruction era, the Pennsylvania native was also a noted clergyman and missionary. Gibbs' son Thomas was also a member of the Florida Congress, and he introduced legislation that would lead to the establishment of Florida A&M University.

The Sunshine Skyway Bridge is technically titled the **Bob Graham** Sunshine Skyway Bridge, and it's so named in honor of Florida's 38th governor. The first version of the bridge, which opened in 1954, was named by a local woman through a Chamber of Commerce-sponsored contest. Its identical twin (1971) was named for W.E. "Bill" Dean of the Florida Department of Transportation. That span was partially destroyed by an errant freighter in 1980, and it was Graham who pushed for the construction of an entirely new, state-of-the-art bridge, of French design, to replace both old spans. He was among the speechmakers at the dedication of the "new" Skyway in February 1987. The history of the bridge is chronicled in *Vintage St. Pete Volume II: Legends, Locations, Lifestyles.*

Boyd Hill Preserve, the city-owned 245-acre spread of woodlands, scrub and hiking trails near Lake Maggiore, was named for 1950s parks superintendent **Boyd Hill**. He was an advocate for leaving this massive wild area wild, for all to enjoy, and it opened to the public – a ong with a small, primitive zoo – after his death in 1957. Boyd Hill's legacy is tracec in *Vintage St. Pete Volume 1 – The Golden Age of Tourism and More.*

There's a life-sized statue (by sculptor Mark Aeling) of **Tony Jannus** on the St. Pete Pier. Jannus, whose name pops up often in St. Petersburg lore and legend, was the pilot who, in 1914, carried the first paying passenger on a scheduled flight (across Tampa Bay, as a matter of fact), thus becoming the de facto founder of commercial airline service. The Jannus story is laid out in full in in *Vintage St. Pete Volume II: Legends, Locations, Lifestyles.*

Jordan Park and Jordan Elementary School are so named to honor **Elder Jordan Sr.**, the city's most prominent and successful African-American businessman. Born into slavery in the mid 19th century, Jordan reportedly bought his freedom at the age of 15. Arriving in St. Petersburg from Columbia County in 1904, he and his sons built not only the Manhattan Casino (initially known as Jordan Dance Hall) but the Black residential community Jordan Park, for which he donated 24 acres. He advocated for and built Jordan Elementary School and – in those segregated times – fought for African-American access to Spa Beach, and a bus line for the Black community. Near the Casino a bronze statue of Jordan, by artist John Hair, was dedicated in 2020. Said Deputy Mayor Kanika Tomalin at the ceremony: "This great man, born into bondage but never enslaved, clearly his soul knew its purpose and refused to yield." *Vintage St. Pete Volume 1 – The Golden Age of Tourism and More* includes the complete story of the Manhattan Casino and its unparalleled contributions to St. Petersburg culture.

North and South Straub Park honor **William Straub**, who historian Walter P. Fuller called "the greatest influence for the development of the community ever to appear on the scene." Editor of the *St. Petersburg Times* for 38 years (he bought the paper in 1901 for $1,300), the Dakota Territory native was a vocal and tireless crusader for better roads, schools and government, and was at the head of the campaign to keep the city's waterfront parks undeveloped and publicly owned. Straub sold majority ownership of the newspaper to Paul Poynter in 1912, but continued as editor until his death in 1939.

Williams Park is named for **John Constantine Williams**. A wealthy landowner from Michigan who relocated to Florida for his health, Williams purchased a good deal of what would become St. Petersburg, and he traded a portion of his holdings to train man Peter Demens, so that the Orange Belt Railway would extend to the area in the late 1890s (the population at the time was less than 100). St. Petersburg was incorporated in 1892.

"When you marry Dixie Rebels with Confederate paraphernalia, that conjures up

Waterfront Park in the 1930s, before it was re-named for Al Lang. City of St. Petersburg

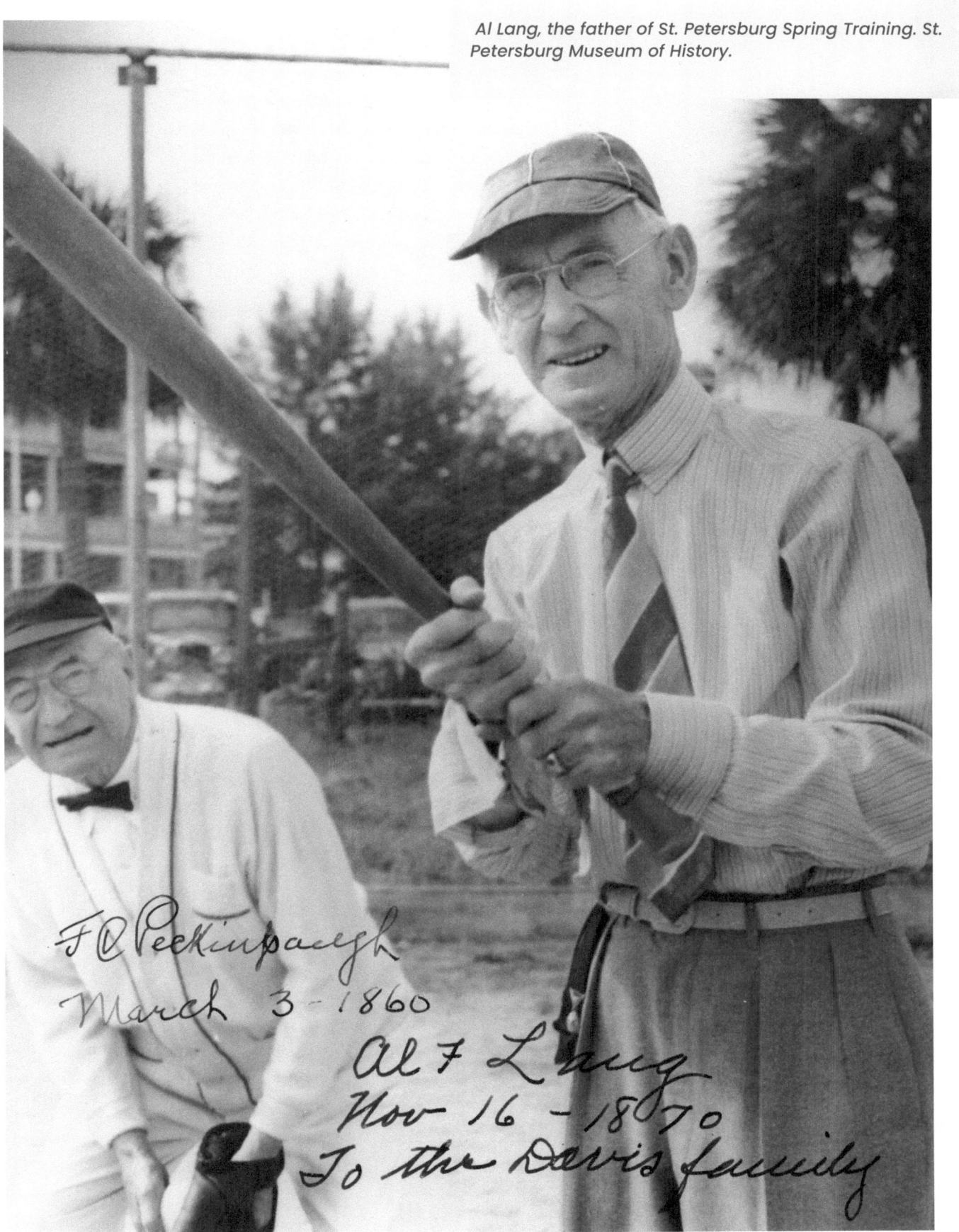

Al Lang, the father of St. Petersburg Spring Training. St. Petersburg Museum of History.

51

a connection to a past, and a racist past," Principal Robert Florio, of St. Petersburg's Dixie Hollins High School, said in 2020. The occasion was the official name-change to Hollins High School; the sports teams would henceforth be known as Royals, rather than Rebels, the name since the school opened in 1959. Namesake **Dixie M. Hollins** had, ironically, been a progressive when he was named the first Superintendent of Schools for Pinellas County in 1912. He argued for better education opportunities for Blacks. Hollins and his family once owned the St. Petersburg Printing Company and the Pasadena Country Club, as well as an expansive cattle ranch near Crystal River. And yes, "Dixie" was his given name.

Nelson Poynter was owner and publisher of the St. Petersburg Times for 28 years. Florida Archives.

Al Lang Stadium was known for many years as Al Lang Field. **Albert Fielding Lang** was the mayor of St. Petersburg from 1916 to 1920, and as such he was part of the booster club of local politicians, developers and businessmen who worked to preserve the city's waterfront park system. But Lang is best known as the man who brought spring training baseball to the city – first the St. Louis Browns, then the Philadelphia Phillies, and the Boston Braves, and then the New Yankees arrived in 1925, staying (with some short breaks) through 1961. Ruth, Gehrig, DiMaggio, Mantle ... all the greats visited St. Petersburg to work out. On the bayfront, the St. Petersburg Athletic Park was demolished, the city erecting an entirely new stadium, bearing Lang's name in honor of his service to the city, and to baseball. When Lang died in 1960, the St. Louis Cardinals were tenured at the ballpark each spring; the team stayed until the arrival of the Tampa Bay Devil Rays in 1998. The stadium was converted into a venue for soccer in 2011, to accommodate the Tampa Bay Rowdies.

The Poynter Institute (for Media Studies), a world-renowned, nonprofit journalism school, was started in 1975 by **Nelson Poynter**, longtime owner, chairman and publisher of the *St. Petersburg Times*. The son of owner and publisher Paul Poynter, Nelson became an editor in the 1930s, and upon his father's death in 1950 was named president and chief bottle-washer. Until his own passing in 1978, Poynter was virtually synonymous with the newspaper (it wouldn't be re-named *Tampa Bay Times* until 2012). He was liberal and he was innovative; he was a powerfully political ally and a vitally vocal civic booster.

North and South Straub Parks were named for early 19th century newspaper publisher William Straub (insert). Park photo: St. Pete Catalyst. Straub photo: St. Petersburg Museum of History.

The Roser Park Historic District is named for **Charles M. Roser**, a developer who moved to St. Petersburg from his native Ohio in 1910. He'd been a confectioner and cookie-baker, and is credited – in some corners – with the creation of the Fig Newton (this has never been verified by Nabisco, which has been turning out Fig Newtons since 1898). The block retaining walls, brick streets, hexagon sidewalk pavers and granite curbstones that made his Roser Park development so unique are, for the most part, still there. However Roser made his fortune, he put it to good use in St. Pete, building (according to historicroserpark.org) the Palm and Poinsettia hotels, Mound Park Hospital, Mercy Hospital, the Roser Park School and other concerns.

Snell Isle (and Snell Arcade) bear the imprint of **C. Perry Snell**. Snell was a millionaire developer from Kentucky who bought his first piece of St. Petersburg – between 1st and 2nd Avenues NE, and between Beach Drive and 1st Street - in 1899. As a resident, he bought up acres of what is now known as Old Northeast, and filled a salty mangrove island to build – you guessed it – Snell Isle, still one of the most upscale neighborhoods in the city. Snell opened the city's first golf course, the nine-hole Coffee Pot Golf Club, in the early '20s (it was later renamed the Sunset Golf and Country Club, and remains today as part of the Vinoy Resort). As a contemporary of William Straub's, he was heavily involved in the efforts to turn the entire bayfront into a series of parks; Snell donated the land between downtown and Coffee Pot Bayou to the city with the proviso it remain green and public.

"The Place to Meet Your Friends"

New Gulfport Casino

at the end of the Gulfport carline
on Beach Boulevard and Shore Drive

Picnics Matinee Dances Balls Tourist Societies Entertainments Ample Parking Space	Open for Bookings John W. Booth Manager Phone 85-485	Refined Orderly Inviting Community Sings on Sunday Attracting Thousands

Built over the Waters of Boca Ciega Bay

Spend the winter with us. Gulfport is located on Boca Ciega Bay, 15 minutes by motor or trolley from St. Petersburg.

The town operates its own city government, has its own water system, fire department, and is one of the most healthful and attractive towns on the West Coast.

Home of F. M. A. and one of the Finest Golf Courses on Florida West Coast

PUBLIC ELEMENTARY AND JUNIOR HIGH SCHOOL
HOTELS, APARTMENTS, ROOMS

FISHING • BATHING • BOATING • SAILING

GULFPORT CASINO
GULFPORT, FLORIDA

The 10,000-square-foot wood-and-brick casino opened in December, 1934. This is a 1940s postcard image.

Center of activity: The Gulfport Casino

There's one question Gulfport Casino manager Justin Shea gets asked more than any other: Where are the slot machines?

The word casino means gathering place, he politely tells guests at the towering, lime green, 88-year-old dance hall on the edge of Boca Ciega Bay. It's derived from the Italian for little house. "We've never had gaming here in the Historic Ballroom, but we are a true casino. An original casino."

Those famous casinos in places like Las Vegas and Atlantic City, he says, in addition to their gambling facilities, have ballrooms, banquet rooms, meeting rooms … at their core, they're gathering places. They're little houses. Over time, the word casino came to implicitly suggest nothing but card games and slots.

Added to the list of National Historic Places in 2014, the Gulfport Casino is almost as old as the city itself. The first iteration was built in 1906, when the salty, sparsely-populated area of southern Pinellas County was known as Veteran City (part of a failed bid to establish it as a retirement community for Civil War veterans).

Top: At the first casino, visitors could step off of the electric trolley from downtown St. Pete directly onto a steam vessel bound for Pass-a-Grille. St. Petersburg Museum of History. Right: The second casino, circa 1922. Gulfport History Museum.

The St. Petersburg & Gulf Railway's electric trolley line had been extended west from downtown, reaching its terminus at Veteran City. Those who wished to visit distant Pass-a-Grille Beach, or fish in blue Gulf waters, would take the trolley from St. Pete and disembark there, climbing aboard excursion boats that steamed across the bay, back and forth, several times daily.

"People forget that there were no bridges then," says Cathy Salustri, a historian, author and owner of the *Gulfport Gabber* newspaper. "There was no Pinellas Bayway, no Corey Causeway. So this was the only way you could get out there."

Veteran City administrators' civic improvement plan included a two-story wood frame building, built atop a pier stretching 800 feet into the bay, with a soda fountain, post office, meeting space and dance floor. The second level was open-air, offering nice overwater views and a welcome break from the generally stifling heat.

It soon became a central destination for residents, who held meetings, pot-luck

Controversial artist George Snow Hill's pirate-themed "drop curtain." Gulfport History Museum.

suppers, parties and even church services there. In time, the railway company conveniently added tracks right on the pier, allowing the beach-bound to step right from the trolley onto waiting steamboats.

The Town of Gulfport was incorporated – the ceremony took place inside the casino – on Oct. 10, 1910. The first Town Hall was erected in 1913; the railroad proper arrived the following year, opening a vein for the expeditious delivery of construction materials just as the Florida Land Boom was beginning.

The hurricane of October, 1921 reduced the beloved casino to a pile of broken boards, and a replacement was hastily erected, on stick-thin stilts over the water.

According to legend, bandleader Camille Thompson once wondered aloud whether the shaky floor might collapse under the weight of so many square-dancing feet.

President Franklin Roosevelt's Works Progress Administration, through the Civil Works Authority, bankrolled an all-new casino building at a cost of $16,000, along with a new fishing pier. Bay bottom was dredged to create the casino site on terra firma, with a protective seawall erected on the waterfront side. Docks were installed to handle the Pass-a-Grille ferry traffic.

Designed by architect Frank Showerman, the 10,000-square-foot wood-and-brick casino opened in December, 1934. It was state-of-the art for its time, with a solid maple dance floor. At the main entrance

The solid maple dance floor, 100×56 feet, photographed in 2022. St. Pete Catalyst.

was a "grand staircase" off Shore Boulevard. Gulf breezes blew in from the large, open window spaces.

At the official dedication ceremony in 1935, 1,200 visitors reportedly turned up to hear speeches about Gulfport's glorious future, and a performance from the Florida Military Academy Band. The military school had recently taken over Gulfport's bankrupt Rolyat luxury hotel (the school would itself sell to Stetson Law College in 1953).

Artist George Snow Hill, who in the '40s created the controversial "racist" mural briefly displayed in St. Petersburg City Hall, painted an historical scene of "Gasparilla and his pirate crew" as the "drop curtain" in front of the band's performance area.

As with St. Petersburg, Gulfport thrived during the winter months, when northerners ventured into Florida to escape the cold. There was a local "society," or club, for nearly every state, and many of them met, celebrated and otherwise co-mingled at the Gulfport Casino.

Always, there were dances, and social hours, and bingo.

And other activities.

A well-to-do St. Petersburg matron was shot to death at 11 p.m. last night near the Gulfport Casino ... held at police headquarters for questioning was Lawrence Minutoli of Tampa, a former Chicagoan ... Showing little emotion but waving his hands in typical Italian gestures, Minutoli said "I go to the dances at the Gulfport Casino often and tonight I was surprised to see her there ... I asked her to pay me the bill she owes me. She tells me there's nothing to talk about, so I shot her. She made trouble for me for 10 years. Now she'll make trouble no more."

St. Petersburg Times/May 13, 1949

The casino has been renovated and upgraded many times over the years. In 1950, the outer façade was redesigned, and a "bandshell"-type stage was added inside; the solid maple dance floor was expanded to 100 feet by 56 feet. Next came acoustic tiles – and, in 1958, the city installed air conditioning. Recessed lighting and chandeliers were added in the 1960s.

The "grand staircase" was closed off, and the main entrance moved to the building's west side in 2003. Extensive shoring-up behind the seawall and concrete support pilings took place, and concrete walkways, with railings, were added.

Manager Shea oversees a staff of three full-time employees and a part-time event staff of 10. The Historic Gulfport Casino Ballroom, as it's now properly known, is fully owned and operated by the City of Gulfport's Cultural Facilities Department, and costs approximately $400,000 per year to run.

The Gulfport Casino looms over the waterfront; it's still the most recognizable – and iconic – building in Gulfport.

"It speaks to a time in our history where we were kind of the end of the line," observes Salustri. "Where people were just starting to come to Florida ... we didn't really have a culture of tourism yet. It was almost like you were in this frontier, because in the '30s Florida was not what it looks like now.

"And then you're going to go to this nice building with hardwood floors, and you'll be able to get a snack, maybe a drink, and they'll have dances or sporting events there, boxing matches, anything like that.

"And you can pretend to be civilized, in the middle of this state that's actively trying to kill you with mosquitos and hurricanes."

The present-day Historic Gulfport Casino Ballroom, opened in 1934 and photographed in 2022. St. Pete Catalyst.

FLORIDA POWER CORPORATION
Presents
Charles Dickens'
CHRISTMAS CAROL
enacted by the
ST. PETERSBURG LITTLE THEATRE PLAYERS

Dickens' famous "Christmas Carol" always portrays vividly the spirit of the Holiday Season. We are pleased to present a radio adaptation of this famous play and are grateful to the Little Theatre Players who are contributing their talent to bring you this appropriate dramatization.

WSUN   **WSUN**

Sunday Afternoon, 2 o'Clock, December 22nd

Cast photo call for the musical comedy "Lil' Abner," March/April 1990. All photos in this chapter: St. Petersburg City Theatre.

Curtain up! St. Petersburg Little Theatre

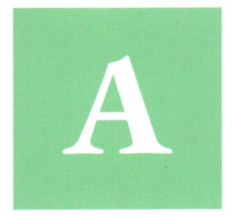fter the turn of the 20th century, small theater companies began to sprout in communities across America, dedicated to putting plays on the stage that defied what was then the norm: Oversized melodramas and rote comedies, surefire-hit touring shows financed by out-of-town producers with cold eyes set squarely on profits, and the baggy-pants follies of vaudeville.

Organized by playwrights, academics and ardent fans of the current European model (experimental plays, news works by new writers, stories that pushed societal boundaries), the "Little Theatre Movement" arrived just as motion pictures were stealing away audiences, to be followed in subsequent decades by radio and television.

Ah, but the theater did not die.

Some of the earliest little theatres were founded by, and staffed with, theater professionals. These morphed into well-known incubators. Many others, those that grew out of ladies' clubs, reading societies and amateur groups, became significant cultural forces in their communities.

Through her association with the St. Petersburg Woman's Club, former stage actress Margaret Beazley established the Sunshine City Players in 1925.

"We offer our services to any organization desiring dramatic entertainment," Beazley's publicity director, Betty Gresh, wrote in a *St. Petersburg Times* editorial. "A real enthusiasm for the drama and a willingness to work and give one's best, are the only requirements for membership in the Sunshine City Players."

Nearly a century later, Betty Gresh's words are still at the heart of St. Petersburg City Theatre's manifesto. Between 1933 and 2010, it was known as St. Petersburg Little Theatre, and although the name and the players – and the plays – have changed over the years, it's essentially the same organization as Margaret Beazley's Sunshine City Players .

Community members join together to put on plays. That's about it.

Actors, directors, producers, stage hands, costume, makeup, lighting, everything that's needed is self-contained (although the play scripts, and there are plenty available, are rented, and royalties are paid).

As St. Petersburg City Theatre's centennial approaches, amateur theater might not be the cultural powerhouse it was in the 1940s and '50s – there are way more distractions these days – but it remains a cornerstone of community life in America. When Mickey Rooney and Judy Garland called out "Hey kids, let's put on a show!" way back when, they were addressing the residents of Anytown, U.S.A.

A theatrical timeline

1933. Now calling itself the Players Club, Beazley's group makes a move to distance itself from its local competitors, including the play-producing St. Petersburg Art Club, by hitching its wagon to the Little Theatre wave sweeping America. On May

9, a new moniker is announced: The St. Petersburg Little Theatre. Directors are chosen and meetings held at the Vocational School. The first two organized shows, *The Poor Nut* and *Outward Bound*, are presented in the Mirror Lake Junior High auditorium.

The SPLT production of the one-act Caleb Stone's *Death Watch* takes first place at the 1934 state Little Theatre tournament

"Post Road," March 1938. The first show produced and directed by "Captain" Patrick Walters.

in Clearwater; by the following year, the contest will be discontinued.

1937. Incorporating as a nonprofit, St. Petersburg Little Theatre hires ex-British Royal Marine "Captain" Patrick Walters, a one-time actor and vaudevillian, as a paid director at $15 per week. Walters, who had married a St. Petersburg woman, told the *Evening Independent* newspaper he would shortly be offering courses in "acting, makeup, designing, construction, painting and stage-managing. Next season, I would like to include three other courses, namely, costumes, lighting and writing."

Walters' hire was to be a game-changer. In a large advertisement for the first play under his regime, *Post Road* (at 35 cents per ticket), the board trumpeted "Our Creed," most likely penned by the incom-

Despite the war (or perhaps because of it) "Arsenic and Old Lace" drew record crowds in January, 1943.

ing director himself: *WE BELIEVE: That the Little Theatre is a definite part of the civic and social life of our Community; that its chief purpose is to afford every individual who really desires it, opportunity for self-expression in the Arts of the Theatre – without thought of payment therefor; that the democratic fulfillment of this purpose makes certain that the drama as an art and an educational and spiritual influence shall not die.*

1942. Walters departs to take care of military business in World War II. Concerned that the public believes their plays are high school productions, SPLT reps go looking for a replacement for the school auditorium, and locate an empty building at 1950 2nd Avenue North, a former grist mill turned upholstery room turned auto-painting shop. The board pays $3,600 for the place, half up front and the rest in the form of a mortgage.

This is when St. Pete started putting the community in community theater:

When it became known that a stage was needed in the old building, the carpenter's union offered to build it. The plasterer's union replastered the outside of the building and, in fact, were so generous that it took very tactful handling to keep them from plastering the inside of the building which would have destroyed the rough unfinished appearance desired for atmosphere. A string of footlights were donated by one of the schools. The American Legion presented 300 seats which they were discarding from an outdoor boxing arena. The plumbers gave their time and material. Definitely not inconsequential were the members who rolled up their sleeves and pitched in.

From "An Early History of St. Petersburg Little Theatre" by Roberta Morrill, 1949

The good fight

The war years proved tough, as young men were in short supply for community productions. And with tires and gasoline severely rationed, fear set in that business would fall off dramatically.

Yet the St. Petersburg Little Theatre was one of the few in the country to remain open, with older men filling in, and the younger ones who weren't overseas – or about to be drafted – recruited for multiple shows per season.

Because several branches of the Armed Forces operated bases for training and physical rehabilitation in the area (specifically, the Vinoy Park Hotel and the Don Ce Sar), there were always soldiers and personnel on the lookout for good entertainment.

A 1943 production of the comedy *Arsenic and Old Lace* (the fifth play in the new building) broke all previous records: "People kept pouring in until they were literally hanging from the rafters," Roberta Morrill wrote. "One player tells of looking out over the footlights and seeing a youngster sitting on one of the ceiling beams." The mortgage was paid off in 1944.

A theatrical timeline – Act II

1955. SPLT's first show for children, *Snow White and the Seven Dwarfs,* debuts with a combination of young and grown-up actors (In the *Times*: "Willa Mae Runyon, seen in *I Remember Mama,* has the role of Snow White … Vince Bouse, new romantic lead at Little Theatre, has the part of the prince.")

The first musical, September 1966: "The Pajama Game."

1957. The board purchases a 3.2 acre lot on 31st Street South and construction begins on an all-new, 250-seat theater building. Total cost is $100,000 – SPLT takes on a $60,000 mortgage – and the custom design includes ample backstage and dressing room space, costume and set storage, and a screened veranda which will ultimately be closed in to create a spacious lobby. The first production, in September 1958, is *Teahouse of the August Moon*

1966. SPLT's first musical: *The Pajama Game*. "Nothing could cheer the heart of a tired businessman more," the *Times* reviewer writes. "Not only are the girls beautiful – but some can drink beer from bottles without removing the cap." Despite such odd plaudits from the local press, the show is a hit, and musicals will

"Once Upon a Mattress," June 1977.

henceforth take up a good portion of SPLT schedules.

1972. A production of the long-forgotten "rock musical" *Your Own Thing*, based loosely on Shakespeare's *Twelfth Night*, is a smash, as is *Hot Pants Revue*, but otherwise sagging ticket sales mean a financial crisis for the theater (not for the first, or the last, time). Dinner theaters, featuring fading show business "names," are all the rage in town. To raise money, old costumes, props and other ephemera are sold off in a garage sale. Tickets prices are raised from $3.50 to $4.

1983. The 1958 mortgage is paid off. Theater classes for children begin.

1994. Major renovations, including a restroom wing to meet ADA standards.

1997. The first "lobby show," the musical *Jung at Heart*.

2005. SPLT hires its first-ever executive director, a paid position.

2011. The name is officially changed to St. Petersburg City Theatre. Year after year, the (mostly) all-volunteer theater is able to meet its meager operating budget through ticket sales, donations, children's camps and the occasional fundraiser.

2017. The wheels fall off. The old "pay-to-play" financial arrangement – keeping just enough money in the till to cover expenses for each show – stops working. The existing board members are tired. Only the youth summer camps are generating money. Amid a pile of debt, the board lets the theater's four paid employees go, and announces that St. Pete City Theatre will close, less than a decade before its centennial.

A group of parents, whose children are involved in SPCT's youth theater programs, convinces the outgoing board to give them a shot at keeping things running, in true Mickey and Judy fashion. "We didn't know what we were doing," says Lisa Marone, part of the original "save the theater" crew. "We just knew we didn't want to see it close."

Just one paid employee is brought back – Kevin Crowell, who works with the kids, the board and the volunteers, builds and paints sets, hauls, carries, repairs, schleps and hustles. Today, he remains an invaluable asset.

2018-19. Approximately $400,000 in repairs are completed at the 14,000-square-foot theater, including a new roof and air conditioning system. Additional upgrades are made.

2020. The theater gets through the pandemic shutdown era with virtual productions.

The good fight continues

Financial difficulties, for any nonprofit, are cyclical (if not constant). The archived paperwork for St. Petersburg Little Theatre is full of dire predictions about the future, that there soon won't be any money, that ticket sales are down, et cetera.

Yet this little theater that could, did. In St. Petersburg, it's King of Rebound Hill.

"I think the history of the theater is so important for us to have, as points of reference," says Marone, whose current title is Fundraising Chair. "To understand that in this somewhat chaotic world that we live in, and the social media that's constantly bombarding us, that we've been here before. We really have. It's just that we have to approach it a different way sometimes. And there's more people watching."

St. Petersburg City Theatre has hit some big bumps along the way, but its title – the oldest continually-operating community theater in Florida – is worn like a badge of honor.

There's a reason, Marone believes, live community theater has endured, and will endure, despite TV and streaming, downloading, video games, social media and the other constant distractions of the era.

It's the human component.

"There's nothing in this digital world that can give you that sustaining feeling of applause when you're onstage," she explains, "and then walking into the lobby and meeting the members of the audience afterwards."

"He Done Her Wrong, or, Wedded, But No Wife," August 1977.

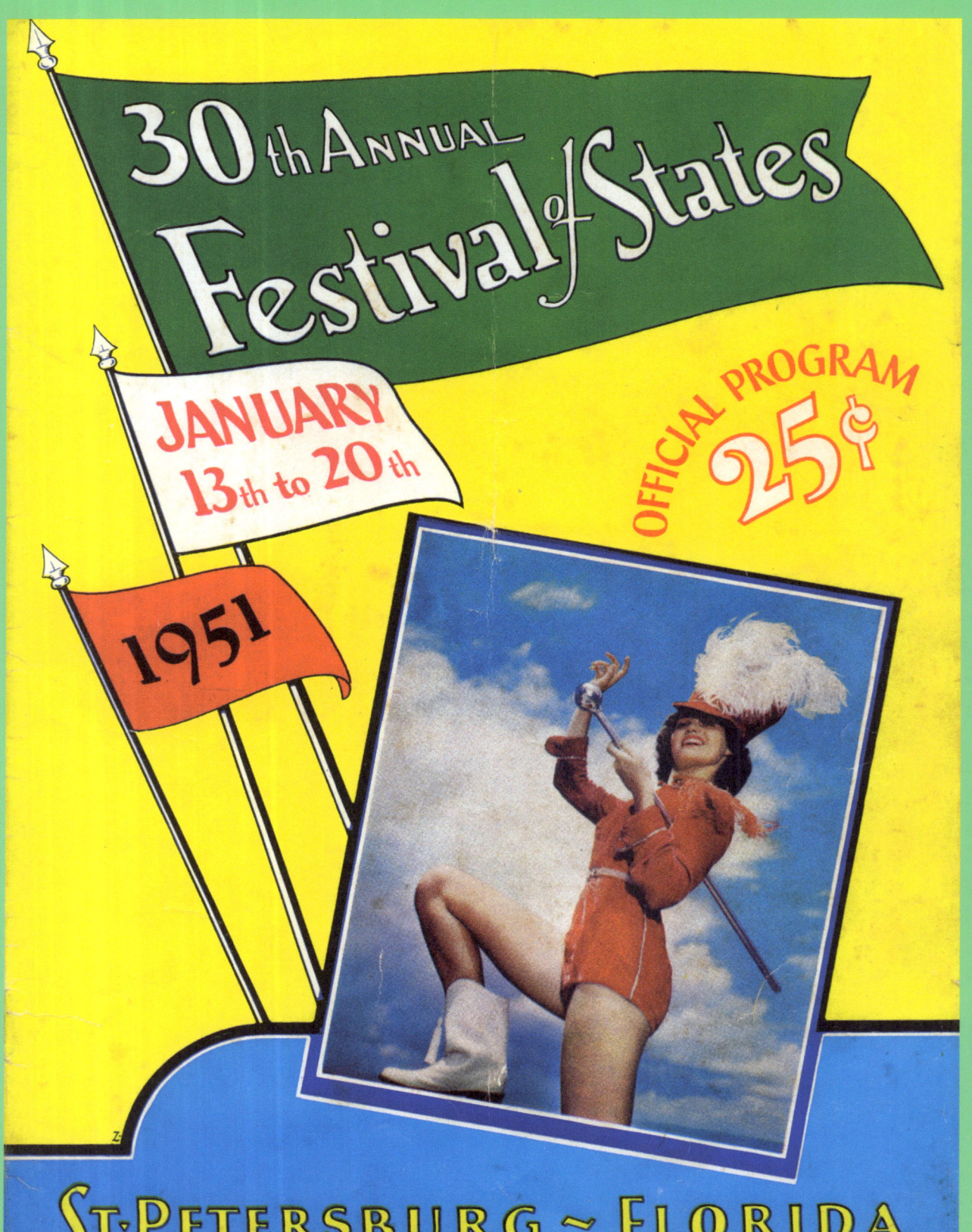

The turn from Bayshore Drive west onto Central Avenue. Postcard image.

Parade Day: The Festival of States

St. Petersburg's journey from provincial town to bustling metropolis can be measured in the story of the Festival of States.

What started in 1896 as a children's celebration of George Washington's birthday turned into a two-week civic festival, always in April, capped off by a parade that at its peak in the 1970s and '80s included marching bands from just about every state in the union. Tens of thousands lined the parade route, up Bayshore Drive from the Vinoy, then west on Central Avenue to 16th Street.

The Festival of States was so named in 1917, when St. Petersburg was a wintering ground for northerners. They tended to arrive in December and stay through March or so, when the weather was warming up back at home.

"What it really was, was a chance for us to extend the season a little bit longer," explains Chris Steinocher, President and CEO of the St Petersburg Area Chamber of Commerce. "To keep those northern dollars down in St. Pete for two more weeks. Try to keep those hotels filled, because it really made a big difference."

Residents of each state tended to gather in tight social groups, so city government and business leaders made appeals:

The 1926 Festival of States Daughters of America float. Florida Archives.

Create a float for your state – and any sort of decorated rolling thing constituted a float – and be a part of our parade.

"It was all about commerce," says Steinocher, "but it gave so many people a taste of St. Pete so that they ended up coming back and living here too. It whet people's whistles so the good ones stayed, and the other ones just left their money."

Although the culminating "Parade of States" was always the big event – in 1923, there were already nine marching bands and 114 floats – the Chamber of Commerce tried a variety of companion pieces, including carnivals, light opera and theater, games, concerts, flower shows, historical re-enactments, lawn bowling contests, animal shows, boat shows, waterski shows, shuffleboard tournaments and the World's Largest Card Party.

The "Coronation Ball," in which a "Sun Queen" was named, began in 1935 (eventually, the crowing of a "Mr. Sun" became part of the party, too).

The festival was put on ice during World War II.

In the mid '50s, a group of local business people formed an all-volunteer group to take the reins. They called themselves the Suncoasters, and they could always be spotted at Festival of States events in their shiny yellow sports jackets.

"Early on, it was a community effort, with a couple of retired guys who had time on their hands," remembers former Suncoaster Joe Lettelleir. "And then they hired an executive director and got organized.

"There were committees – a parade committee, a security committee, a hospitality committee ... you got on a committee depending on your wishes, or who you knew in the hierarchy, and you worked on different things, from the Kids' Parade to the Clown Alley."

Although the city kicked in a stipend, it was up to the Suncoasters to secure enough sponsorship dollars, and contributions, to make the Festival of States hum like a well-oiled marching band machine.

As a volunteer, "You had to be civically involved, and working for a company that would allow you that time off," Lettelleir says. "And of course they were happy to have you do it; you were representing them."

In 1973, the National Civic League named St. Petersburg an "All-America City." This prestigious designation was trumpeted by the *St. Petersburg Times*, which every spring published a Festival of States special edition.

Former Councilmember Barbara Gammon was quoted: "It is entirely fitting that the young people who come here to

A 1948 Festival of States float from Aunt Hattie's restaurant. Postcard image.

A parade perspective (1960) along Central Avenue, with the Coca-Cola Bottling Company and WFLA-TV sportscaster Marty Foster. Flickr.com/electrospark.

The Northeast High School Marching Band on Bayshore, 1972. Florida Archives.

show off their musical talent, resplendent uniforms and marching ability demonstrate what our All-America City entry showed, that people can work together in achieving a common goal for the good of all."

In this same section was an editorial, under the headline *We Think We Are the Greatest, But We Know We Have Problems*:

We're not proud of our ghetto, for instance. If you live in a decaying northern city, our ghetto wouldn't impress you as all that bad, perhaps, nothing like you've seen in New York or Chicago or Detroit, or Cleveland. But there is still substandard housing near the heart of our city ... despite this, the voters turned down a Public Housing Referendum last month.

The bigger St. Pete got, the less relevant the Festival of States became.

"For a long time, the banks were all local, and they were happy to be a sponsor," says Lettelleir, who left the Suncoasters in the mid 1980s. "Then there came a time when the banking decisions were all made out of Atlanta and Charlotte and Jacksonville. So you didn't get the commitment."

When family-owned business were the norm, he adds, "It was the big civic event, and everybody had a stake in it one way or another, from street vendors to balloon salesmen to everything else. And a lot of things changed."

Cable TV, home video, the internet, cell phones and the arrival of the Tampa Bay Rays all made standing around in the springtime sun watching floats and high school bands parade down the asphalt seem somehow quaint, as archaic as the celebrity dinner theaters that thrived in St. Pete in the 1970s and died out completely by the end of the next decade.

With far less support from area businesses, dwindling attendance and the arrival of the St. Petersburg Grand Prix, which turned downtown upside down, the Suncoasters retired the Festival of States parade in 2014. The group itself disbanded four years later.

Steinocher, a longtime resident of St. Pete, remembers the sense of civic pride that came with each April's iteration of the Festival of States. "It was not a government-funded thing," he says, "it was the community going 'Hey, let's put on a show so these people will come back next year. It was another one of those personal commitments to leave them wanting more of us.

"That's what I was impressed by. It was a personal thing to show people how cool St. Pete really was."

Above: Sears Roebuck department store's float in the 1960 parade. Flickr.com/electrospark. Below: Float from "Imperial Polk County" in the 1966 parade. St. Petersburg Museum of History.

Tom Reese, 1957. "One usually does the thing one loves to do," he told the St. Pete newspaper on Feb. 17. "I get my kicks out of pushing other artists and their work, and my gallery comes before me as a passion." From the collection of Mari Eliza.

Reese and his beloved Beaux Arts Gallery and Coffeehouse, 1993. "It is difficult to explain the attraction the Beaux Arts had for so many young men and women back then, especially to a generation captivated with laptops and iPods," David McCullum wrote after Reese's death in 2006. "Tom Reese gave us a safe place to gather, where we could escape the rules of our parents' generation and feel comfortable expressing our own opinions." Tampa Bay Times/Zuma Press.

The Beaux Arts Gallery and Coffeehouse

Tom Reese told the author of *On the Road* to hit the road.

Legendary beat novelist Jack Kerouac, living out the last alcoholic years of his life in mid-1960s St. Petersburg, was known to frequent the Beaux Arts Gallery and Coffeehouse, the ramshackle bohemian outpost Reese operated next to the north-south railroad tracks in Pinellas Park.

Kerouac would sit in the back of the dark, high-ceilinged room, smelling of mildew and stuffed helter-skelter with stained easy chairs and ratty sofas, and listen to the poets and the folksingers. The writer was known to carry a flask of bourbon in his jacket pocket.

"Tom knew damn well who Kerouac was," recalls musician John Balcomb, who lived for a time upstairs in one of the Beaux Arts rooms-for-rent. Reese told him the story a dozen times. Maybe a hundred.

"And Kerouac really appreciated Tom, because the Beaux Arts was a little bit of San Francisco, right there in St. Petersburg, just a conservative retirement town at that time."

The Royal Palm Hotel, built by Tom's uncle Howard Reese in 1911. From the collection of Boo Ehrsam.

But for all the creative freedoms allowed and encouraged at 7711 60th Street N, butting up against the Pinellas Park police station, Reese maintained a handful of ironclad rules. According to Balcomb, "Kerouac was usually too loaded to do his own poetry. Or maybe he didn't want to do it.

"But the last time, Tom escorted him to the door and threw him out. He said 'I don't put up with people drinking in my establishment.'"

Thomas Bruce Reese (1917-2006) was eccentric, opinionated, fiery, driven, and openly gay. He was also a man of eclectic tastes and extreme talents, an accomplished painter with a BFA from Stetson University and an MFA from California College of the Arts, a journalist who wrote art criticism, a published poet and a dancer who'd performed with Ted Shawn's world renowned all-male company.

He was a Renaissance man who pointed the arts in Pinellas County towards its future.

A Navy postmaster during World War II, Reese had immersed himself in the art, theater and dance scenes of several large European cities, working and studying. He was also a voracious reader.

It was 1950 when Reese returned to Pinellas Park, where he'd lived, with his mother, since the age of 4. He took a job as a mail carrier for the town.

Tom and "Mother" lived in a small house behind the Royal Palm Hotel, built in 1911 by his uncle Howard. She inherited the property – the tin-roofed hotel, the house and the garden – when her brother-in-law died.

Reese immediately set about turning the old clapboard structure into the launching pad for his dream: A progressive art gallery and an art school. There was to be nothing like it in the area.

His co-founders at the Contemporary Arts Gallery and College included sculptress Maybelle Muttart Faldareau and painters David Anderson, Ted Powell and Sydney Stein. Among other accomplishments, Stein had designed the classic circus-train box for Animal Crackers, and the bright red packaging for Ritz Crackers.

Although Reese and the artists in his orbit continued to give art lessons for much of the '50s, the original plan didn't pan.

"Students on the GI bill were precluded from attending his art school," explains San Francisco artist Mari Eliza, who knew Reese later in his life. "That basically killed it for him. So he had to switch, from what he wanted to do, to something else."

And so began the poetry readings and the folksingers' nights, in the main gallery room, or outdoors in the garden. Art contests were regularly scheduled and proved extremely popular with the locals, with regional and even national artists.

He turned another downstairs section of the Royal Palm into the "movie room," where he programmed foreign and experimental, "avant garde" films.

Maria Eliza was a Tampa teen, disheartened by what she perceived as the universal conformity of her peers, and whole-heartedly uninterested in the pop music on the radio. When she was introduced to the coffeehouse crowd, she says, "I felt really comfortable with the people. I didn't realize how weird I was until I discovered people who were weirder than I was. I started going there on a really regular basis."

For free spirits, there was one, and only one, place to go.

It was most likely the fall of 1961 when Jim Morrison, still six years away from stardom as the charismatic frontman for the Doors, wandered into the Contemporary Arts Gallery and Coffeehouse.

A student at St. Petersburg Junior College, the scruffy Morrison was obsessed with the poetry of Rimbaud, and the writings of Nietzsche and others who questioned the accepted way of things (he was also a big fan of Jack Kerouac, but it's unlikely the two ever crossed paths).

In 1963, not long after he left Pinellas County – and the Beaux Arts – for Tallahassee, Jim Morrison was arrested for disturbing the peace (i.e. being drunk and obnoxious during a football game). He was 19 years old. Wiki Commons.

According to Reese – and he told the story to anyone who would listen – Morrison, 17 or 18, got onstage and read his own poetry, with his back to the audience. On numerous occasions.

Reese's friends insist he exerted great influence on the future rock star.

"Tom would explode on people," recalls Balcomb, "and that's what Morrison was copying on the dramatic parts of his

Left: Scenes from the Sarasota Beaux Arts Balls, where Tom Reese was a regular visitor (collection of the author). Right: Reese with "Miss Edna" at one of his Pinellas Park parties. From the collection of Chris Skillman.

Doors records, where he would go from singing to screaming. Tom infused him with a lot of theatrical stuff."

There was something else, according to Pinellas Park artist and longtime Reese confidante Boo Ehrsam. "Tom advised him he should keep his junk on the outside of his underwear, under his pants. To get more attention."

Belle of the balls

There was, to be sure, nothing conventional – or staid – about Tom Reese. He loved costumes, the more outlandish or revealing the better, and won several prizes at the Sarasota Art Club's annual Beaux Arts Ball. He began producing Beaux Arts Balls himself, as fundraisers for his own organization, in St. Petersburg.

Theme of the ball is "Primitive Urge," and costumes suggestive of Indian and frontier life are suggested as easy and appropriate. Judge of costumes, according to Thomas Bruce Reese, Contemporary Art Gallery director, will be Baron Sepi Dobranyi, famed sculptor, art director and film producer.
St. Petersburg Times/March 13, 1960

It was 1962 when the Contemporary Arts Gallery became the Beaux Arts Gallery, re-named for Reese's beloved costume balls.

"I went there many times as a teen and young adult in the late '60s and early '70s," Kristin Lindh says. "When I told my mother where I was going, she related a story of Tom having a New Year's Eve costume party where he appeared with peacock feathers attached to his rear-end and wearing nothing else."

"Every Friday or Saturday night," recalls Balcomb, "he would go to a place in Tampa he called The Baths. He would get all dressed up. He would gargle with some weird mouthwash; you could smell it all through the place. And he used some kind of a cream or ointment on himself, which had a very strong odor, too, when he walked by you."

It was commonly known among the boarders and coffeehouse regulars that Reese held after-hours parties, in the second-floor room he kept for himself, with male visitors.

"Halloween was unbelievable," Balcomb says. "My jaw dropped. I would sit by the front door and watch the characters coming in. All these gay guys in these outfits, and women, too, that were accompanying them. In these outlandish outfits, wearing almost nothing. Feathers all over them and stuff like that."

In November, 1961 – around the time young Jim Morrison was hanging around – Reese was arrested for "crimes against nature," and given five years' probation. He was acquitted of "lewd and lascivious conduct" in 1964. Run-ins with the police, over the explicit nature of some of the films he screened, continued through the decade. He laughed them off.

He caused a scandal when dancer Bob Achlin, dressed in barely-there Indian attire, was featured dancing on a coffee table just inside the front door.

"Apparently," Boo Ehrsam says, "Pinellas Park blamed him for the '60s."

'Walk like a ballet boy'

Reese enjoyed being the center of attention; a natural storyteller, he would hold court between folksinger sets and describe the afternoon in 1961 when Marilyn Monroe, vacationing on Redington Beach with ex-husband Joe DiMaggio, came into the gallery and bought an "outre" painting.

Or the time Allen Ginsberg dropped by. Or Gamble Rogers, or Will McLean or Bobby Hicks – Florida folk music legends all – or when Fred Neil and Vince Martin played a set. Or Jerry Jeff Walker, from Greenwich Village. Or Tampa's Henry Paul (soon to rocket to fame with the Outlaws).

Then there was guitarist Danny Finley, whose successful band Bethlehem Asylum literally formed on the Beaux Arts stage.

He was the first in the county to show Andy Warhol's underground films, and to screen John Waters' controversial *Polyester*, complete with "Smell-o-Vision" scratch 'n' sniff cards.

"Tom was not shy, and he would brag

openly that he had the oldest coffeehouse in the south," says John Balcomb. Anyone could come and perform – it was the St. Pete area's first "open mic" club.

Although you paid the modest admission at the door – Reese's ancient mother handled the cashbox – the coffee was free, and it was bottomless. Absolutely no drugs or alcohol allowed.

Unless, that is, you were boarding in one of the old hotel's upstairs rooms. "There were a few transients – guys that just wanted a cheap room," Balcomb says. "But the others that lived there were musicians. We used to leave our doors open, and there was always guitar music. People were always smoking a joint and playing guitar. During the week, it was so placid and quiet. You'd go down into the garden and walk around. It was just an ethereal place to hang out at and live."

Still, he adds, "I'm sure he was bi-polar. He had a very, very intense personality. He knew everything about art, and all the greats and all that. If you were talking to him, he would tell you stories, he would talk about the sexual proclivity of different people. And he would always talk about Morrison.

"And then, if you had asked a question of Tom, he would flip out on you. Even strangers, like a husband and wife that came in to see the gallery, he would be very nice and cordial at first, and then he would just snap out and start yelling YOU'RE NOT LISTENING TO ME! YOU HAVE TO LISTEN TO ME! Just totally manic."

Balcomb, who's writing a book about Reese and the Beaux Arts (to be titled *The Source of the Madness*), says that even those who saw Reese every day never quite got used to his sudden mood swings.

"He would scream at you in the gallery if you were walking upstairs with your boots on, clomping up the steps: WE CAN HEAR YOU ALL OVER THE HOUSE! His voice would go into a falsetto. YOU HAVE TO WALK LIKE A BALLET BOY!"

'A center of creativity'

The end began in 1977, when fire took out the music room (the building was not insured). A dozen years later, a bigger fire did irreparable damage to the upper floors (the building was still not insured).

Reese battled Pinellas Park government over code violations, permits and unpaid taxes. The Pinellas Park City Council bought the property for $162,000, paid off the back taxes and liens and razed it to the ground in 1994 – the same year, ironically, the Pinellas County Arts Council gave Reese its "Friend of the Arts" award.

Boo Ehrsam, whose friendship with Reese solidified and intensified in the late '80s, says that like a lot of creative people, he just wasn't very good with money. The crowds had already dwindled perilously low by the time of the second fire.

"He tried lots of things, and sometimes it worked and sometimes it didn't," she recalls. "Musicians are really great, but that didn't mean that the people who attended had money. That's part of the problem. The people who knew him forever maybe donated a little, but they were retirees. Or young people who appreciated being there, but just didn't have the money."

By this time, there was competition, as St. Petersburg was starting on its belated journey to arts mecca status.

"When we opened 44 years ago, there wasn't a gallery in Tampa or St. Petersburg," Reese crowed to the *Tampa Tribune* on opening day for the "new" Beaux Arts, in downtown in St. Pete.

"There's no smoking or drinking here, so there's no fuss about age. Both the young and the old will be able to mingle together. The place will be so lively and entertaining nobody will even be tempted to smoke."

Reese vowed to let a little sunlight into the new location, in stark contrast to the dark and dank of its predecessor. "At my age," he said, "I can say to hell with the trash. I'm going to run a very elegant place."

Announced City Councilman Ernest Fillyau, a photographer who'd first exhibited his work at the Beaux Arts in the 1950s: "Pinellas Park's loss is our gain."

Although it lasted nearly a decade, the downtown gallery and coffeehouse never was much of a success. The times they were a-changin.' The magic was gone.

Reese died in a Clearwater nursing home Jan. 19, 2006, of complications from the diabetes he'd neglected for years, at the age of 88.

In her letter nominating Thomas Bruce Reese for the Arts Council Award, Boo Ehrsam effectively summed up what her friend and mentor had done for St. Petersburg:

Tom has put aside his own aspirations to contribute to the arts as a facilitator, instructor and muse. He gave Pinellas County a center of creativity before the Dali, Museum of Fine Arts and the PCAC. He created a much copied format for gallery/coffeehouse facilities. He has helped to mold great talents. Tom Reese kept this area from becoming a cultural wasteland, encouraging all creative efforts. The people who passed through Beaux Arts, and those who were touched by Mr. Reese's influences, are better for it.

Boo Ehrsam describes Reese's chosen appearance, towards the end of his life, as his "Walt Whitman look." Photo by Mari Eliza.

Tarpon Springs diver and shopowner John Gonatos had a small part in the 1948 movie "16 Fathoms Deep." Florida Archive.

Anastasios "Taso" Karistinos has been sponging out of Tarpon Springs for more than 50 years. 2022 photo: St. Pete Catalyst.

The Tarpon Springs sponge industry

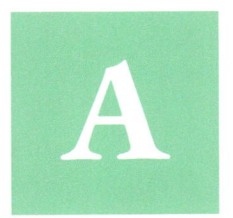At one time, it was said, there were so many sponge boats in Tarpon Springs that you could walk from one side of the Anclote River to the other without getting your feet wet.

The first Greek sponge divers arrived in 1905, lured by the calm Gulf waters that so mirrored their life-giving Mediterranean.

The sponge is the exoskeleton of a sedentary, plant-like animal that clings to rock and bottom. Divers in Western Greece had been efficiently collecting sponges for centuries, walking the coastal floor dressed in weighted rubber suits and heavy copper diving helmets, connected to the sponge boat via a length of metered-out air hose. They brought their techniques, and their traditions. to the United States.

By 1920 there were more than 1,500 Greeks living in Tarpon Springs, and more than 200 boats making the trip out the Anclote and into the Gulf, where they'd remain for days, weeks, even months at a time clawing sponges from the seabed with a short, pointed rake and stuffing them into mesh bags.

They raised their families there, went to church, sent their kids to school. They opened coffee shops and bakeries and restaurants devoted to Greek delicacies. They branched out into other areas of business, and the city blossomed.

Sponge Exchange with Sponge Docks in background, 1921. Burgert Brothers photo/Tampa-Hillsborough County Public Library System.

At the Tarpon Springs Sponge Exchange, distributors, wholesalers and mercantile dealers came from all over the world to bid on great lots of Tarpon Springs wool, yellow and vase sponges. And by the mid 1930s, Tarpon Springs had not only survived the Great Depression, it had prospered. The local sponge industry was a $3 million business.

A global sponge blight crippled the industry in the 1940s and '50s, and although the sponges came back, periodic red tide blooms and man-made pollution still took a toll on sponging. As an economic driver, sponging never recovered.

Tourism is the number one industry in today's Tarpon Springs, which has more Greek residents, per capita, than any other American city.

Anastasios "Taso" Karistinos, 69, owns one of the six commercial sponge boats still operating out of Tarpon Springs. He's not rich, he admits, but he makes a decent living.

Karistinos was 19 years old when he left the Greek Island of Evia to live and work

in Tarpon Springs. He is divorced, and his 46-year-old son Anastasi operates Sponge Divers Supply, not far from the Sponge Docks where Dad keeps his boat, a 46-foot fiberglass classic Greek model, also called *Anastasi*.

His son, Karistinos explains, has three children of his own. "I don't want my grandkids to do what I do," he says. "This is a dangerous, risky job. I did it because I had no choice. I spent so much money, I built that boat and then, you know what they say, you gotta dance the way the music plays."

Sponge diving is the music he knows. A sponger can't go out alone – there has to be at least one other person along, to drive the boat when the red-and-white "diver down" flag is aloft.

"I got 800 feet of air hose, and I can go anywhere I want on the bottom," explains Karistinos. "I have an orange buoy behind me, and the boat follows the buoy. I don't know where the boat is. I just go anywhere I think there are sponges, and the guy on the boat has to follow that buoy.

"And that's how we communicate – if I pull down one time and let it go, that means I want to come up. I pull it twice down, plop, one behind the other, that means I want another bag."

The bulky helmets were long ago traded in for skin-diving masks, although the air hose is still connected to a compressor onboard – spongers don't have much use for portable air tanks. And the sponges are cut from the seabed, rather than plucked or raked, to allow the animal to regenerate.

"Younger people are more attracted to their electronics. They don't want to go sponging, because it's physical. Sponging is hard work. A lot of sleepless nights. Bad weather. They're not into it because they have so many options on the land. Why should they go do this hard work with somebody like me? I'm a pirate. I don't know how long I'm going to be out there – I can stay a month and still I don't care."

Local boys, he laments, "we can't keep them a week out there, they get sick. Everything bothers them. They want to be home.

"In order to make good money, a good living out of this, you got to stay out more than two weeks. Right after two weeks you start making the money."

Monetizing Tarpon Springs' cultural significance was the primary goal of New Yorkers Lou and Eileen Rozee (nee Rosenblatt), who landed in the city in 1969. The couple purchased the lot at 510 Dodecanese Boulevard, adjacent to the Sponge Docks, and created the first (and to date only) tourist attraction devoted to the Greeks and the salad days of sponging.

Beneath its corrugated aluminum roofs, Spongeorama included a restored 90-foot, two-masted schooner of the type used as a mothership by early spongers, along with a free movie on the history of sponging, from Ancient Greece to the present day, which played on a continuous loop. Gift shops and a "Greek Village" were added.

Sponging is better in deeper water, but the risks from "The Bends" (the decompression sickness that can kill a diver if he surfaces too quickly) are also greater. For longer trips, and into deeper water, a larger crew is necessary. And, Karistinos admits, good crewmen are getting harder to find.

Taso Karistinos swears he remembers a shallow pool, into which a suited-up diver would descend, and emerge with sponge in hand, to the delight of visitors.

Many remember the walk-through history tour, featuring a series of dioramas – life-sized historical scenes – behind thick panes of glass. Originally, you could push a button and hear the voice of a narrator.

These tableaus combined 2-D painted images of divers, seagrass, fish and real sponges, next to depictions of Greek village life using department-store mannequins in vintage costumes, and one unforgettable scene of an unfortunate fellow who'd suffered "The Bends." The diver-mannequin was clearly dead, rivulets of painted-on "blood" flowing from his mouth and nostrils, as his shipmates looked on with pained expressions.

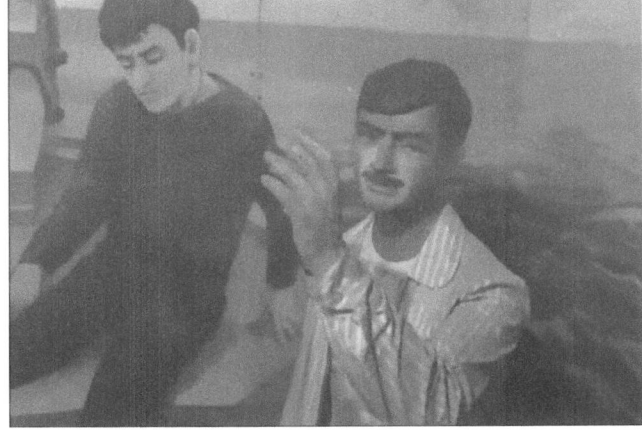
Spongeorama diorama (detail), behind glass, 2015. Collection of the author.

Next to this tragic scene was a hand-painted sign:

SPONGE DIVING: PROBABLY MOST DANGEROUS OCCUPATION IN UNITED STATES

 – Newsweek Magazine

L.B. Rozee, who'd been a travel writer, journalist and radio and television host, was smitten with Tarpon Springs. It was largely through his efforts that the Sponge Docks were designated a National Historic Landmark in 1972.

That year, Lou and Eileen self-published the guide book *Sponge Docks, Tarpon Springs Florida: America's Sponge Diving Birthplace*.

Spongeorama expanded in the early 1970s, with a small hotel, a coffee shop and additional shops and boutiques. The Rozees' boats took visitors on sightseeing cruises up the Anclote and into the Gulf.

When they retired in 1982, and sold the property, Lou and Eileen proudly told the local newspaper that half a million people visited Spongeorama annually – even more than nearby Weeki Wachee Springs, they said.

Time, however, wasn't kind to Spongeorama, and as the decades passed, along with a succession of new owners, one section after another was closed and its contents sold off.

By 2017, the diorama mannequins, with their painted-on hair and shiny black ethnic moustaches, were literally rotting. People came just to laugh at their faded, rat-gnawed remains.

They were finally retired after Hurricane Irma sent a surge of water and wind up the Anclote and into their glass-fronted chambers.

Today's Spongeorama consists of a

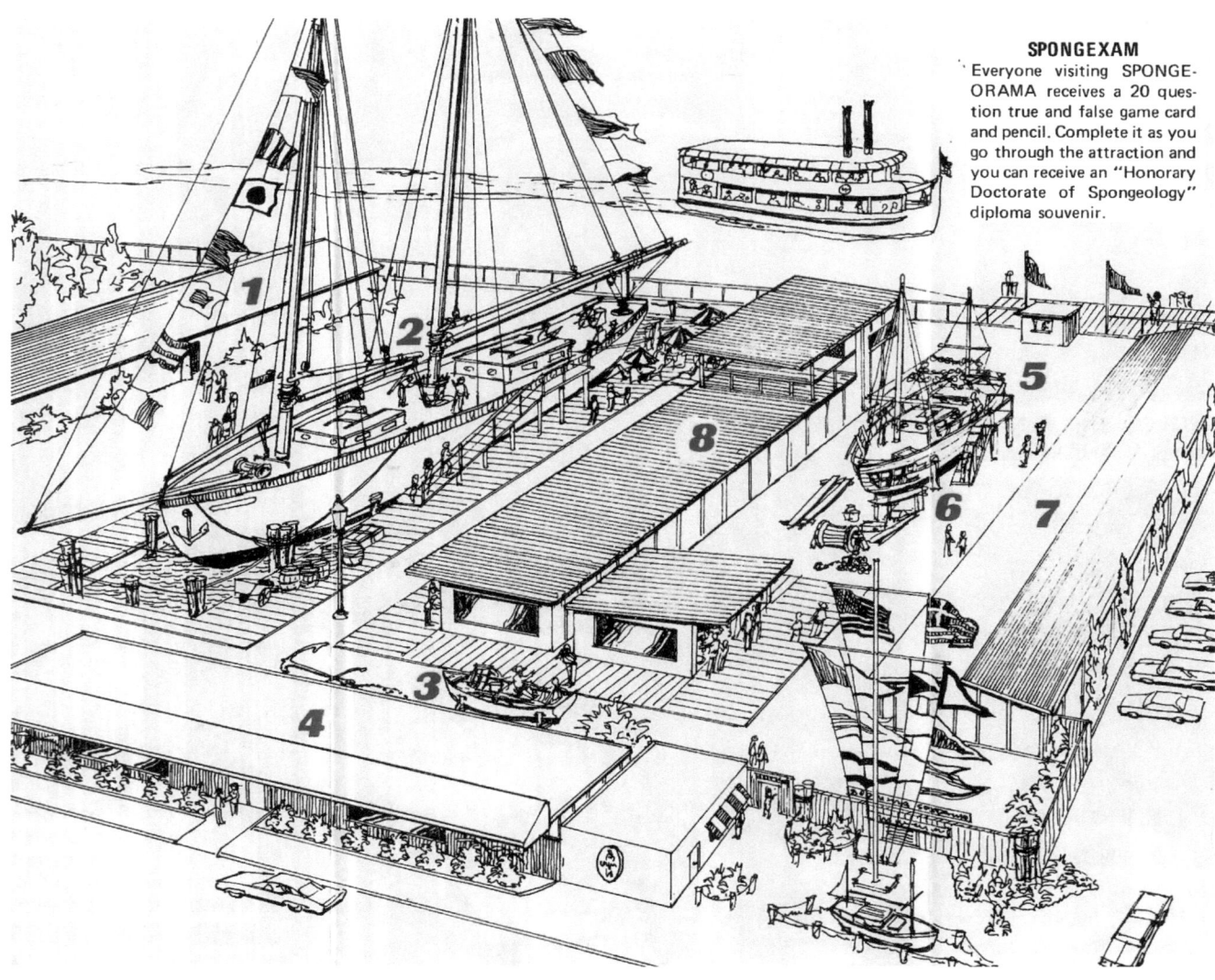

Spongeorama tourist attraction site map, 1970s. Collection of the author.

single gift shop, along with a successful excursion boat business, with sightseeing and dolphin cruises on the river and out into the Gulf.

And somewhere in the back of the gift shop, in a mildewed room behind a creaky black door, the 1970s sponge movie is still going on a continuous loop – all day, every day.

Tina Bucuvalas is president of the Greektown Preservation & Heritage Association. A veteran folklorist who spent a dozen years as the head of Florida Cultural Resources, Inc., she is writing a book about the Tarpon Springs sponge industry.

As the cost of fuel and supplies have gone up, she explains, the price for natural sponges has not. Add to that the lack of enthusiasm for the old ways among Tarpon Springs' young people, and as the old-timers age out, the lifestyle and the profession are dying.

"No one has encouraged members of their family to go into the sponge industry for decades and decades," she sighs. "I'm afraid there's not going to be people replacing them, unless something changes drastically."

Among the gift shops dotting Dodecanese Boulevard on both sides, she explains, most of the natural sponges they sell come from local boats. But sponges harvested in the Bahamas are a small percentage. In a final stroke of irony, American distributors – including those based in Tarpon Springs – are selling Bahamian and local sponges to Greece, where they constitute the majority of sponges sold in tourist stores.

It's all about the tourists now. Taso Karistinos, who was given the Florida Folk Heritage Award in 2010, says he might retire one day, but he's certain the legacy of sponging will remain central to life in Tarpon Springs.

"Always, somebody's going to be here, bring in some sponges just for show," he says. "But it's not going to be glory days."

A returning diver is helped out of his helmet, circa 1910. Burgert Brothers/Florida Archives.

Tarpon at the movies

The 1948 Hollywood melodrama *16 Fathoms Deep* opens with the wheezing door of an old passenger bus. Out steps Lloyd Bridges, a duffel bag over his shoulder. He looks up and down the street, and says in a voiceover:

When my trick in the Navy was finished, I got to talking around. Somebody mentioned a place in Florida. Tarpon Springs. I never heard of it. Big sponge-fishing place, biggest in the world. Lots of work for divers. I still never heard of it.

Also starring Lon Chaney Jr., *16 Fathoms Deep* fictionalized the story of Tarpon Springs. It was shot there, too, in glorious black and white, right on the docks and along Dodecanese Boulevard.

Although the underwater scenes were done at Marineland in St. Augustine (Watch out for that giant killer turtle!), *16 Fathoms Deep* includes lovingly long shots of the old wooden docks, and of

A lobby card for 1948's "16 Fathoms Deep" with Lloyd Bridges (left) and Lon Chaney Jr. Collection of the author.

boats going in and out of the Anclote.

There's the original Sponge Exchange, long before it was developed into a quaint collection of gift shops, seen in action as "captains" haul their "prize sponge catches" into the central courtyard for auction.

Take away the sappy love story, the hammy acting and the bad-guy shenanigans, and the movie – a remake of an inferior 1934 film of the same name – displays a startling authenticity vis a vis the process of divers "suiting up" and dropping into the water.

Tarpon Springs was also ground zero for the filming of 1953's *Beneath the 12-Mile Reef,* one of the earliest movies shot using the widescreen Cinemascope process. Gilbert Roland stars as a Greek sponge diver named Mike Petrakis, whose hot-headed teenage son Tony (Robert Wagner) wants to wear the rubber suit, and the helmet, and Be Like Dad.

There are several scenes showing Dodecanese Boulevard and the original Sponge Exchange, and since the movie (unlike *16 Fathoms Deep*) was shot in color, there's a vivid crispness to the images (the underwater scenes for this one were shot in the Bahamas). And both movies accurately depict the Epiphany, the century-old religious ceremony held each January at Spring Bayou.

Yet *Beneath the 12-Mile Reef* plays out like a seagoing *West Side Story*, as opposing sides square off – the Greeks vs. the Conchs – with Wagner and Terry Moore as the sponge-crossed lovers, and a cameo appearance in the final minutes that stretches the already-thin limits of believability.

Two words: Giant octopus.

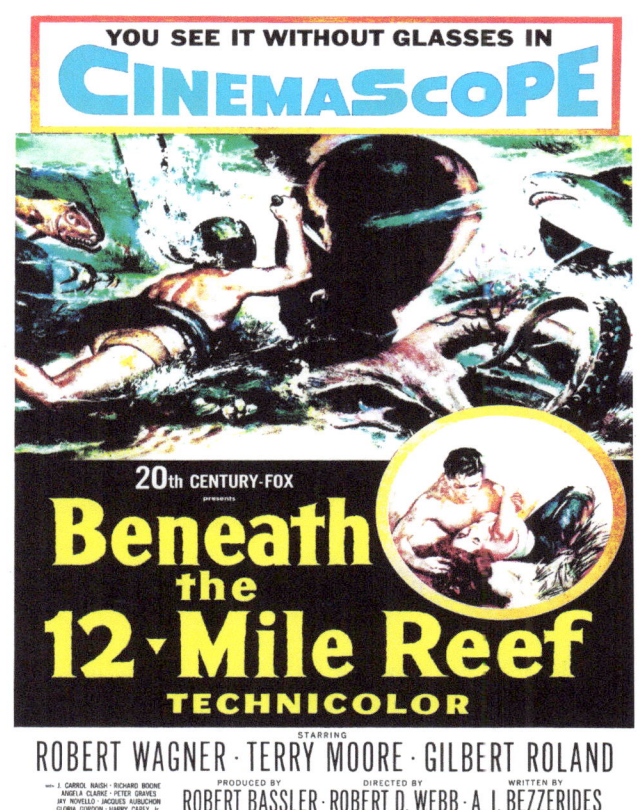

Below: J. Carroll Nash, far left, assists diver Robert Wagner in a seagoing scene from the 1953 Cinemascope potboiler "Beneath the 12-Mile Reef." Columbia Pictures.

Architect William Harvard designed the five-level "Inverted Pyramid" Pier, which opened on Jan. 13, 1973. Rockne Krebs' laser light sculpture debuted – or was supposed to - March 20, 1976. City of St. Petersburg.

Krebs himself took this photograph of The Laser, then a work in progress, from the approach to the pier in 1975. @Artists Rights Society.

The Pier, The Laser and Rockne Krebs

s a City of the Arts, St. Petersburg's road from "provincial" to "powerhouse" was long and bumpy.

The reception to public art, in particular, was chilly long before Janet Echelman's *Bending Arc* was proposed for the new St. Pete Pier in 2018, producing the expected outcry from citizens who just didn't see why the City, or anybody, should spend thousands of dollars on a big, blue fishing net suspended from tall white poles.

The Echelman sculpture is, of course, considerably more ambitious and artistic than that, and today it's a major part of the Pier experience. People grew to accept the large-scale art, and they grew to embrace it.

Things didn't go so well for internationally renowned sculptor Rockne Krebs, who was commissioned in 1974 to create a piece for the then-new "Inverted Pyramid" pier. After dodging the slings and arrows of public bewilderment, and scorn and outrage from City Council and others in local government, Krebs delivered "The Laser" on budget, and on time. On March 20, 1976, he flipped the switch to give St. Petersburg its first look at the city-owned state-of-the-art, ahead-of-its-time laser light sculpture.

And it didn't work.

"Everything about this piece was very

Another photo by the artist: "Star Board: Home on the Range, Part VI," the operations center on the third floor of the pier. @Artists Rights Society.

new, and even to this day there are very few people who really understand the whole aesthetic of it," remembers Glenn Andrews, who was the director of the city's Arts Commission (and Krebs' project director) in the mid '70s.

Lasers, or focused beams of laser light, were relatively new at the time, especially as components in artwork. The moving parts of Krebs' creation, which sent a green beam westward over 2nd Avenue NE and another over downtown, were housed in a clear plexiglass box Krebs named Star Board, on the third floor of the Pier.

The beam's mate fired in a pattern towards a series of prisms and mirrors, mounted on light poles, trees and buildings, which split the green shaft into different directions, shapes and colors in a repeating black-sky light show.

The Laser (and the Star Board installation, which naturally refracted and redirected rainbow lights behind it, throughout the third-floor space, every sunset) worked intermittently before Opening Night.

Dressed-up dignitaries gathered inside the Pier, sipping laser-green cocktails, while a crowd of 1,400 assembled on the long approach to watch the official debut of the Krebs creation.

Its failure on that warm spring night was blamed on a tiny replacement part that had not arrived, from the west coast, on time.

Rockne Krebs was so named by his father, a sports fan, after college football great Knute Rockne. The St. Louis native was a pioneer in light sculpture and held several patents for laser technology.

"Lasers, and their appeal, made sense for where his art was in the 1960s," says Heather Krebs, who has managed her father's archives since his death in 2011. "He was always working with light and with transparencies. His sculptures were transparent plexiglass, and everything had to do with space and lines, and the absence of the material still made up the art.

"The empty space around the plexiglass sculptures were part of how he visually saw the art and the lines. And I think that the lasers just made so much sense to him – being able to create those lines on a much larger scale."

Krebs created his first three-dimensional laser sculpture in 1968, and began crafting urban environmental sculptures, using lasers, shortly thereafter.

"His drawings were amazing," remembers his daughter. "He could draw anything. And to be able to draw in space, I don't know how he could turn that down. Who could turn that down?"

Krebs couldn't turn down an offer from St. Petersburg's mayor and the newly-formed Arts Commission to develop something for the city's new Pier (the "Inverted Pyramid" went up in 1973, replacing the antiquated Municipal Pier).

Rockne Krebs oversees his work. City of St. Petersburg.

The National Endowment For the Arts granted $20,000 for Krebs' Pier sculpture, and City Council approved an additional $25,000.

Barely.

Dreama Dawson reminded councilmen to the applause of the audience that "there are people waiting all day long in the unemployment line. We have no money." She urged the council to first consider "the basic needs of humanity."

"To draw a line at this time would basically be to ignore the last 40 years when we've done nothing for the arts," replied Mayor C. Randolph Wedding.
        St. Petersburg Times/Feb. 21, 1975

Local newspeople, Anderson believes, didn't know "beans from bullets" when it came to accurately describing Krebs' work, and what it did. Laser art was in its infancy, and there was an entirely new palette of words to be learned.

"The main laser beam would go right over the top of 2nd Avenue, all the way out and actually out into space at that point," he says. "There were reports of people out in the middle of the Gulf of Mexico that saw that green thing go over the top. And were stunned by the whole thing."

The laser would kick on right at sunset, as a subtle reminder of Florida's famous "flash of green," the natural phenomenon that occurs at the moment the sun "sinks" into the Gulf.

The Star Board installation was part of a national series Krebs called "Home on the Range." (St. Pete's was subtitled "Part VI.") He had decorated it with beach sand, a tiny palm tree, a plastic flamingo and other Sunshine State ephemera.

When The Laser was working, said Anderson, it was "otherworldly and the eighth wonder of the world. But when it was broken down, it was a curse."

Until it was dismantled and removed in the mid '80s, it was barely operational.

Nevertheless, Anderson says, "I have always been thrilled to have been involved in that project, and to having been around Rockne. He was an extremely brilliant artist. And when you understand

Krebs and his 5-year-old daughter Heather in St. Petersburg. "He'd spend months measuring and figuring out how to make things happen," she says. Krebs family collection.

the processes of that installation, you see the genius.

"I sat down there with him and watched him doing some drawings and thinking things out. I wouldn't have missed that for my life."

Heather Krebs was 5 years old when her dad was in St. Petersburg working on The Laser. She remembers it well. "Depending on where you viewed the laser piece, different shapes were happening in the sky," she says. "Different drawings. Different light sculptures in the sky.

"He'd spend months measuring and figuring out how to make things happen. And sometimes magical things happened."

An otherworldly postscript

Two years after Rockne Krebs died, rumors began flying among online UFO enthusiasts that "proof" of a close encounter, in St. Petersburg, had been documented back in the '70s.

The source was a mysterious folio of fanciful sketches depicting laser beams, a tornado and drawings of "aliens" and a five-headed beast, along with a handwritten description of the "incident."

The material had been discovered on the side of a road in Asheville, N.C., and when its contents were uploaded to Reddit, the online community went ballistic with speculation.

Tampa Tribune reporter Paul Guzzo spoke with Asheville resident Dan Wickham, who'd uploaded the material at the behest of a "friend." It was all very mysterious.

"He obviously saw something that changed him," Guzzo quoted the man as saying, and noting in his story that July 7, 1977 – the date referenced in the material – a tornado had touched down in Pasco County. Add to that phenomenon "mysterious" lights in the sky over St. Petersburg … voila, "evidence" of UFOs in Florida.

"I can't believe this is happening,' said Heather Krebs when contacted by the *Tribune*. "It's all so bizarre. My father was not into UFOs, but he would have loved this."

A crew member from the Coast Guard Cutter Bernard C. Webber pays his respects at the memorial for USCGC Blackthorn during a 2017 ceremony. Photo by Petty Officer 1st Class Michael De Nyse.

USCGC Blackthorn was one of 39 original 180-foot seagoing buoy tenders built between 1942 and 1944. United States Coast Guard.

The US Coast Guard Blackthorn tragedy

As ships go, the United States Coast Guard cutter *Blackthorn* was diminutive: Just 180 feet from bow to stern, and 37 feet abeam, with a displacement tonnage (weight) of 984 tons.

By comparison, the tanker *Capricorn*, which rammed and sank the World War II-era buoy tender January 28, 1980 in Southern Tampa Bay, was a leviathan, weighing more than 14,000 tons, and stretching 605 feet lengthwise, and 75 feet from port side to starboard.

Capricorn was also carrying 151,611 barrels of viscous No. 6 fuel oil that day, inbound for the docks at Weedon Island.

Blackthorn, with a crew of six officers and 44 enlisted crewmen, many of whom had never gone to sea before, was leaving Tampa, where it had been in drydock – for repairs and upgrades – since October. The sailors were excited to finally be underway; the first stop would be Mobile, Alabama, followed by a short sail to Galveston, Texas, *Blackthorn*'s home port.

The Coast Guard ship started its outbound transit at 6:04 p.m., precisely at sunset. Two hours and 17 uneventful minutes later, *Blackthorn* and *Capricorn* collided, bow-to-bow, just west of the Sunshine Skyway Bridge.

Within a matter of moments, the smaller vessel capsized and sank to the bottom of the shipping channel, drowning 23

103

Jan. 29, 1980: The morning after. Capricorn rests, self-grounded, as the clouds of silt and diesel fuel on the water are all that remain of Blackthorn. Tampa Bay Times/Zuma Press.

crewmen. It remains the worst peacetime disaster in Coast Guard history.

Why did it happen? How did it happen? The facts are these: The temperature over Tampa Bay was 61 degrees on the early evening of Jan. 28, 1980, with a light wind out of the north. Seas were calm.

For ships, passage in and out of Tampa Bay consists of a series of marked channels, dredged to specific depths to allow for vessels with deep drafts (the amount of hull below the waterline) to move without grounding. The majority of the bay is naturally shallow, 12 to 13 feet.

In a way, these channels are like roads, and all watercraft traffic, regardless of size, must adhere to the maritime rules of the road. At its most basic, this boils down to a single directive: Stay in your lane.

A Soviet cruise ship, *Kazakhstan,* had just left the Port of Tampa and was making its way through the labyrinth of dredged passages towards Mullet Key Channel, the main "road" on the seaward side of the Sunshine Skyway Bridge. Initially *Blackthorn* was ahead of the cruise vessel, and also overtook and passed a slow-moving tugboat, *Pat B*, pushing a barge.

Kazakhstan, brightly lit with red, blue, green and white deck lights, then increased speed, and the harbor pilot aboard radioed for permission to pass

Blackthorn. Permission was granted and the cruise ship moved around and ahead without incident.

In the moments before *Blackthorn* approached Cut A, a dogleg turn under the Sunshine Skyway that would quickly straighten out into the main channel, Commanding Officer George J. Sepel, 34 had handed the conn (control) of the cutter to his Officer of the Deck, 29-year-old Ensign John Ryan.

Determining a ship's exact position, and the position of potential obstacles, is a scientific process using radar, strategically placed lookouts, terrestrial point fixing, astronomy, range lights, deck lights ... and common sense. It's much harder after dark. Without a fixed horizon at which to compare distances and sizes, the human eye is fallible. Perspectives are unreliable.

None of the lookouts on the cutter's forecastle (raised bow), nor on the flying bridge, knew *Capricorn* was in the short channel ahead of them and moving in their direction. They were transfixed by the bright lights of the towering *Kazakhstan*.

Once *Blackthorn* cleared the Skyway, Sepel looked at the radar screen and observed a "large radar contact" turning into Cut A. At the window, Sepel, Ryan and the executive officer saw the blinding lights of *Kazakhstan* – and a larger, darker shape emerging from beyond its port side.

Aboard the tanker, harbor pilot Gene Knight observed that *Blackthorn* appeared to be keeping to the center of Cut A, and not to the right side, its designated "lane." Knight tried to contact the Coast Guard vessel but received no reply. "What's this guy trying to prove?" asked *Capricorn*'s captain George McShea.

Sepel then stepped out onto the port bridge wing of *Blackthorn* and beheld the giant tanker bearing down on his little ship. "Where the f–k did he come from?" he exclaimed.

It was obvious to pilot Knight that a standard port-to-port passing was not going to be possible. He issued two short whistle blasts, indicating that he would attempt an unorthodox starboard-to-starboard pass. *Blackthorn*'s course did not change, and Knight – out of options – sounded four whistle blasts – the danger signal.

Sepel ordered Right Full Rudder, automatically taking back conn of his ship. "Stand By For Collision" was piped, Sepel put the engines back full ... and the two vessels hit.

Knight stopped his engines, but the forward motion of *Capricorn* continued. One survivor testified that he saw sparks, like someone was welding, as the ships' metallic sides slid and grated together. *Capricorn*'s seven-ton port anchor became embedded in *Blackthorn*'s side, ripping a massive hole in the head and shower area belowdecks. Four feet of anchor was later found embedded in the showers.

Knight ordered his rudder hard aport, to avoid drifting into the Skyway Bridge, and the engines full astern. But the ship continued forward until the anchor chain pulled taught. And so Blackthorn, listing to port, was dragged, backwards, like an uncooperative dog on a rope.

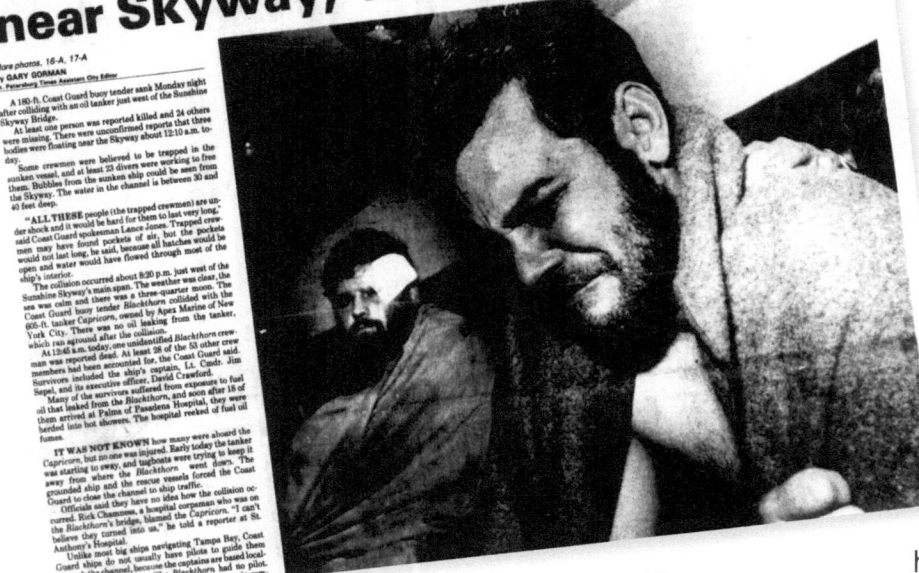

All was pandemonium aboard the cutter. Rookie crewmen scrambled to a bulletin board to check where they were supposed to be during an emergency. It was discovered that several of the life rafts were not in inflatable condition; not that there would have been time. Several crewmembers later testified that they didn't know how to inflate the rafts, anyway.

When the chain reached its "bitter end," with *Capricorn* still in motion, the tug caused *Blackthorn* to violently roll and go belly-up. Sepel shouted "Abandon Ship," and crewmen began jumping into Tampa Bay. And the vessel sank on the edge of Cut A Channel, in approximately 40 feet (the dredged depth) of 64-degree water.

"I could see two men in the water that was bubbling up," Quartermaster 1st Class Jeff Huse testified. "I was washed aft. I was caught by cable across the stomach. I was drug down with the ship. I freed myself and fought to reach the surface.

"Upon reaching the surface I saw the hull upside down. Water was spewing out ... it was spraying on me. I was looking for a place to hang onto ... a man reached out and grabbed me. The man turned out to be the captain."

It came to light that there had been a hero amidst the calamity: Seaman apprentice William R. Flores, an 18-year-old Texan, located the starboard lifejacket locker and began throwing lifejackets over the side to fellow crewmembers in the water.

As the inverted vessel began to sink, Flores used his belt to tie open the locker door, and continued distributing lifejackets, as well as aiding shipmates in distress.

His body was among the first recovered when rescue teams descended on the site that night.

In 2000, Flores was posthumously given the Coast Guard Award, the highest non-combat bravery award the service can bestow. Eleven years later, a new cutter was named the *SS William Flores*.

Blackthorn was raised via barge and crane on Feb. 19. Fourteen bodies were found inside the wreck.

Incoming and outgoing ships had been forced to navigate a temporary channel, beneath the Skyway, while the sunken cutter rested on the bottom. As soon as *Blackthorn* was successfully floated and removed, normal shipping resumed.

It was determined that the cutter was a total loss; it was later scuttled in the Gulf of Mexico to create an artificial reef.

When his turn came to testify, *Blackthorn* CO Sepel – fearing he was to be held to the fire – gave his rank and number, then declared: "Sir, under the advice of my attorneys, I am invoking my rights under Article 31 of the Uniform Code of Military Justice and I respectfully refuse to answer your questions."

Later, after days of legal back-and-forth, Sepel was offered the opportunity to re-think his response; he then spent five days on the witness stand.

Major changes were to come, according to Rear Admiral W. F. Merlin USCG (ret.). who was Deputy Controller of the United States Coast Guard in Washington, D.C. in 1980. "As a result of the investigation," the now Tampa-based Merlin says, "the Coast Guard took several actions requiring prospective commanding officers, and perspective executive officers,

Feb. 19, 1980: After three weeks at the bottom of Tampa Bay, the Coast Guard cutter Blackthorn is raised. Tampa Bay Times/Zuma Press.

to take a special course, offered by the Navy, in emergency ship handling. Which heretofore had been recommended but not demanded.

"Also, a selection process: The other thing was they established boards for review of the backgrounds of potential COs. This independent panel reviewed their backgrounds to determine whether they were recommended to be CO or not."

Before he took command of *Blackthorn*, Sepel had not been aboard a ship for five years.

The National Transportation Safety Board put the blame on Sepel, for allowing an inexperienced sailor to conn the vessel in unfamiliar waters, in heavy traffic. In its conclusion, the report said "The Safety Board can only conclude that these officers did not know where they were."

The Coast Guard's Marine Board of Inquiry concluded that "the proximate cause of the casualty was the failure of both vessels to keep well to the side of the channel which lay on their starboard side."

"I believe," says Merlin, "in the final analysis, the conduct of the *Blackthorn* was at least ninety-nine percent at fault. And if you hold the ship at fault, the CO is responsible for the conduct of the ship."

Both CO Sepel and Ensign Ryan narrowly averted court-martial; instead, through a legal procedure known as an Admirals' Mast, Sepel was given a letter of admonition, to be placed as a permanent entry in his military record – the lightest possible punishment for an officer.

Ryan received a similar letter.

Every Jan. 28, the United States Coast Guard holds a memorial ceremony at the site of its Blackthorn memorial, at the rest area on the north (Pinellas) side of the Sunshine Skyway.

Bill Merlin has sat on the memorial committee for decades. The full-dress ceremony, he stressed, is significant in several ways.

"These were innocent people who lost their lives in the service of their country. They couldn't be held responsible for the accident. So it's a memorial to them – let's make sure that those 23 lads are not forgotten.

"But the secondary purpose of holding it is to remind everybody of the dangers of going to sea if you're not fully prepared, and not following the regulations, et cetera, that were designed to prevent accidents like that from happening. It's an annual reminder for the entire Coast Guard that we need to be careful out there."

With the loss of 23 sailors, *Blackthorn* was the worst disaster visited upon Tampa Bay – for 102 days. On May 9, during a blinding, unanticipated squall, the 606-foot freighter *Summit Venture*, approaching the Cut A Channel turn at almost exactly the same spot as *Capricorn* before it, was blown off-course and collided with the Sunshine Skyway Bridge, causing the deaths of 35 motorists whose vehicles plunged 150 feet into the water below.

SEMPER   PARATUS

USCGC BLACKTHORN WLB-391
28 JANUARY 1980

SS1	SUBRINO I. AVILA	1 MAY 1948	PALIWAS, R.P.
SNGM	RANDOLPH B. BARNABY	27 JAN. 1958	DETROIT, MICH.
MK2	RICHARD D. BOONE	22 SEPT. 1956	PATTERSON, CAL.
SA	WARREN R. BREWER	21 JUNE 1961	MEMPHIS, TENN.
QM2	GARY W. CRUMLY	22 JUNE 1956	BIRMINGHAM, AL.
DC2	DANIEL M. ESTRADA	25 FEB. 1957	LOS ANGELES, CAL.
EM2	THOMAS R. FAULKNER	2 JULY 1957	BONNETERRE, MO.
SA	WILLIAM R. FLORES	6 NOV. 1961	CARLSBAD, N.M.
SS3	DONALD R. FRANK	22 JULY 1956	BEAUMONT, TEX.
DC3	LAWRENCE D. FRYE	20 JAN. 1959	CLARKSBURG, W. VA.
QM3	RICHARD W. GAULD	28 MAR. 1960	YOUNGSTOWN, OH.
SA	CHARLES D. HALL	11 APR. 1958	TEHRAN, IRAN
SA	GLEN E. HARRISON	1 APR. 1961	CORDOVA, AK.
MK1	BRUCE M. LAFOND	9 JUNE 1947	HOLYOKE, MA.
FA	MICHEAL K. LUKE	6 JUNE 1959	CHICAGO, ILL.
MK1	DANNY R. MAXCY	22 SEPT. 1954	MOBILE, AL.
SA	JOHN E. PROSKO	25 JUNE 1960	STEUBENVILLE, OH.
ET1	JEROME F. RESSLER	7 SEPT. 1951	BISMARCK, N.D.
CWO2	JACK J. ROBERTS, JR.	8 FEB. 1941	LAFAYETTE, LA.
SA	GEORGE R. ROVOLIS, JR.	11 AUG. 1962	SAVANNAH, GA.
ENS	FRANK J. SARNA	16 JUNE 1957	CHICAGO, ILL.
EM3	EDWARD F. SINDELAR, III	8 JAN. 1959	CHICAGO, ILL.
MKC	LUTHER D. STIDHEM	11 JAN. 1940	SEQUIN, TEX.

MOURN NOT FOR HIM
HE SAILS WITH ONE MORE DIVINE

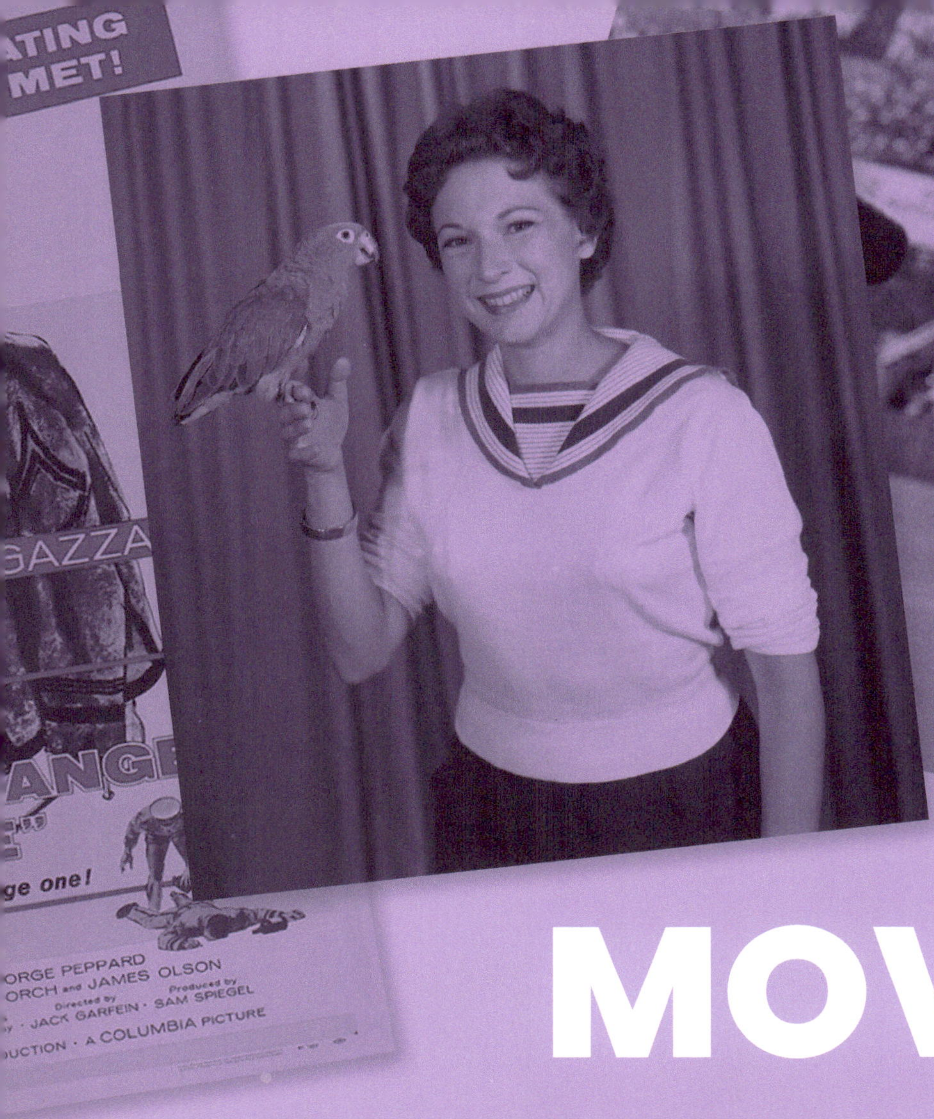
ATING
MET!
GAZZA
ANGE
ge one!
ORGE PEPPARD
ORCH and JAMES OLSON
Directed by
JACK GARFEIN
Produced by
SAM SPIEGEL
UCTION · A COLUMBIA PICTURE
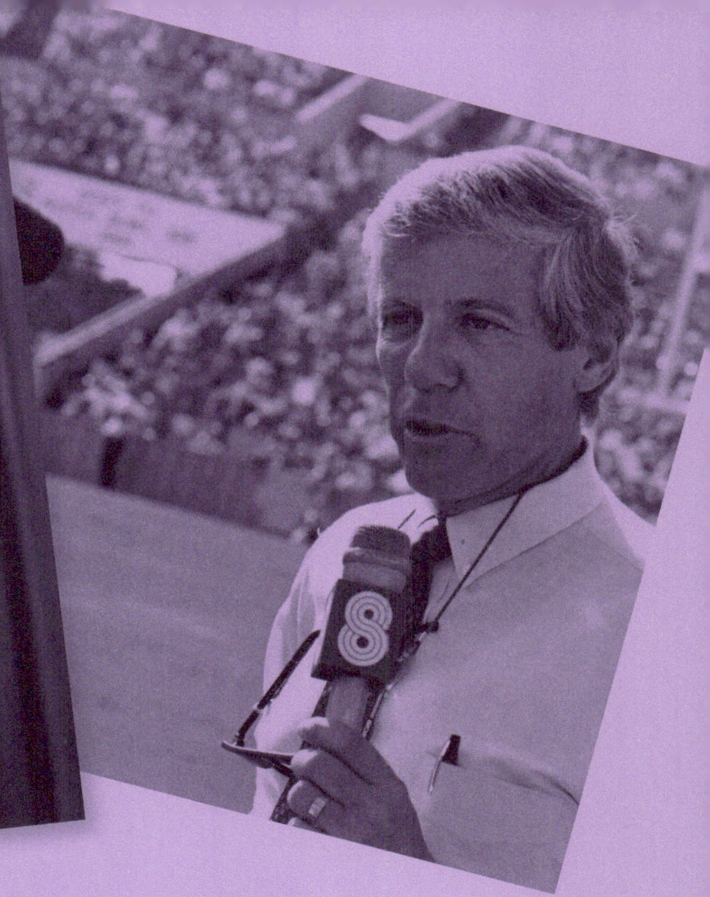
8

MOVIES & TV

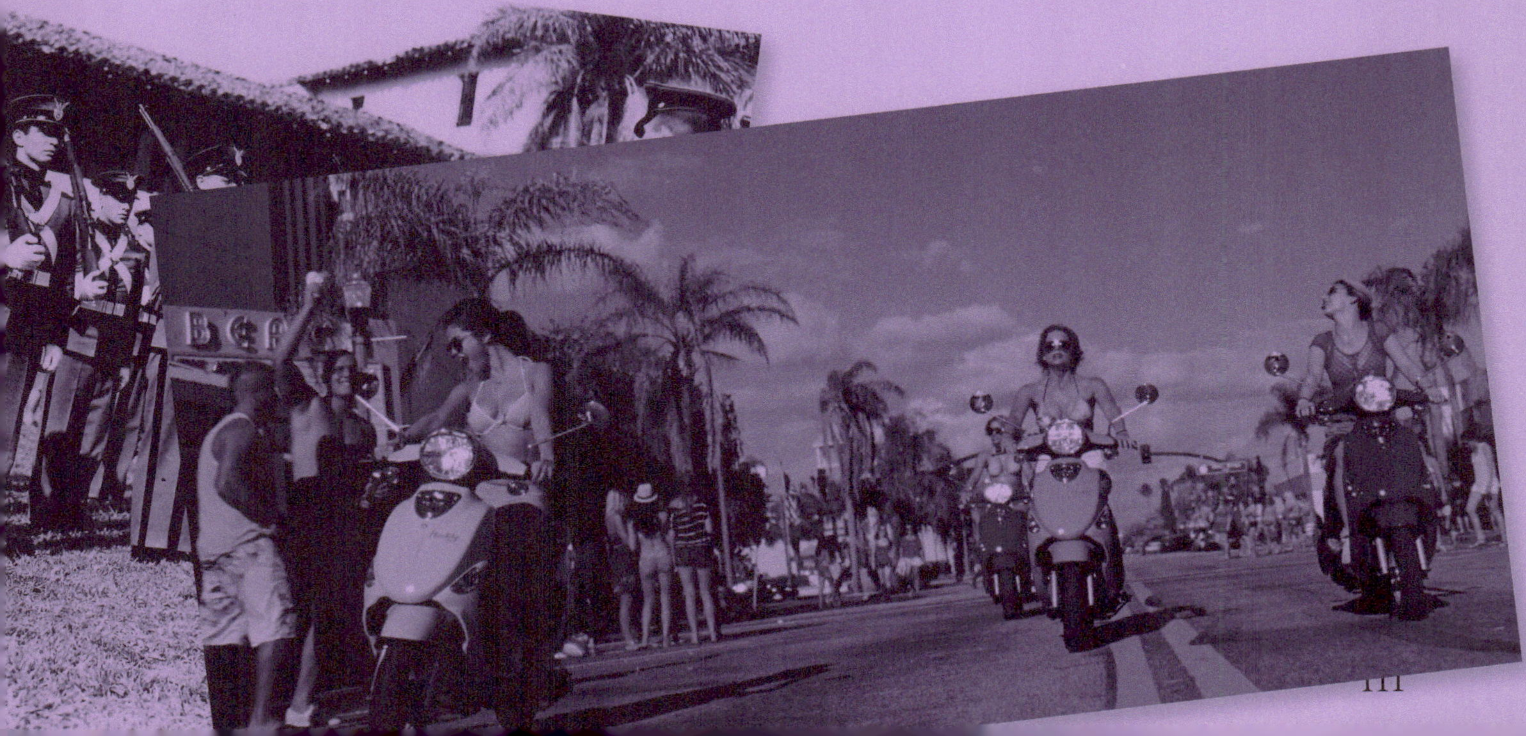

Singer and guitar player Ernie Lee (Ernest Eli Cornelison) was one of Tampa Bay's first TV celebrities.

"Salud, and happy days." Manuel Beiro and Andy Hardy, every Friday night between Pulse News and "Shock Theatre." All images in this chapter from the collection of Mike Clark.

The WTVT Big 13 family album

ust give me Dixie, where folks are smilin'
And all the while invitin' you there.
Where friends will greet you, say 'I'm glad to meet you'
Sunshine is everywhere.

Every weekday at 7 a.m., bay area residents turned on their TVs to this welcoming song from friendly-faced singer and guitar player Ernie Lee. The show, on WTVT-Channel 13, was *Good Day*, and it was the station's bacon-and-eggs sunrise programming from 1956 until the early 1990s (by then, it had been re-titled *Breakfast Beat*).

Ernie Lee's country music, interview segments and corny hillbilly jokes were interspersed with news, sports and weather. In the 1960s and '70s, before CBS had its own morning show, *Good Day/Breakfast Beat* regularly out-performed rival NBC's *Today Show* (broadcast locally on the competition, WFLA-Channel 8). Ernie Lee was one of Tampa Bay's first big stars.

The network took an hour for *Captain Kangaroo*, but otherwise the morning belonged to Ernie and his friends.

Until the arrival of cable television in the 1980s, there were, in essence, just three channels in the bay area, one for each national network. The on-air personalities at WTVT – or Big 13, as it nicknamed itself – were some of the most recognizable residents of St. Petersburg and Tampa.

The WTVT studios at 1113 Memorial Highway, Tampa. This road was re-named Kennedy Boulevard in 1964.

Big 13 was Number One in the ratings for 25 years, between 1962 and 1987.

The Fox network took over management of WTVT in 1994, and the morning show, in a different form, still exists (as *Good Day Tampa Bay*). For the generations who came of age watching Big 13, however, "local TV" means Ernie, Salty Sol, Roy, Mary Ellen, Paul, Shock, Andy, Hugh and handful of other indelible personalities.

Channel Thirteen, we're on the Gulf in sunny Flor-i-da!
People know us, and they watch us
Get today's news today
See it fresh all the way!
Channel Thirteen, we're CBS for Suncoast Flor-i-da!
We will give you much more
Of what you're looking for
And it's all seen on Big 13!

Ray Blush

Ray Blush, who'd been a reporter, news director and the creator and host of the groundbreaking *Project 13* documentary series (as well as the host of the high school game show *High-Q*) is literally the last man standing from those early, all-important days.

It was, Blush said, "The best of times. Because today the whole journalism industry has changed. It was just a lot different back then – socially, morally, economically, you name it."

It was easy to identify with the men and women you saw regularly on TV. Tampa Bay was a much smaller community, and when these people came into your home, day after day, you were generally happy to see them.

They were happy to be there together. "We were not only working professionals, side by side, we really were a family," reflected Blush. "We had a family atmosphere there. We were friends and we did a lot to help each other along the way. And we did a lot out in the community. It was a wonderful experience."

Salty Sol Fleischman

Sol Fleischman was a known commodity when he was hired by WTVT in 1957, replacing original sports director Guy Bagli. He'd been a popular sportscaster for WDAE radio, and wrote a fishing column in the *Tampa Times* (which is where he acquired the nickname "Salty Sol").

Gregarious and fun-loving, Fleischman's folksy personality came through on his daily forecasts – he appeared on *Good Day*, the noontime *Pulse Plus* and the 6 p.m. evening broadcast.

He was an avid boater who lived to fish, and his evening segments featured "Salty's Best Bets," educated predictions and suggestions for the next morning's fishing.

"Salty Sol" Fleischman in action.

"He was anything but the slick, slim, good-looking master of ceremonies sort of anchor," explained his son, Tampa architect Sol Fleischman Jr. "He was always fat, he was baldheaded, but he just had a way. He was charismatic and he loved to talk to people. He loved people."

And people loved him. Fleischman pioneered a bit called "Where Am I?," in which he'd show a snippet of silent film of someplace or other in Tampa Bay. The viewer who guessed correctly won a prize (reportedly, one week 5,000 cards and letters arrived at the station).

Salty Sol, who'd grown up in Plant City, had always been passionate about sports. "Back in his early days, he was quite an accomplished high-board diver and swimmer in high school," said Sol Jr. "Legend says he swam around Davis Island with some famous swimmer, while he covered it for the radio."

At home, Dad was "just like he was on TV.

Salty Sol's deputy, and successor, Andy Hardy

Bigger than life."

And he was especially popular with children, who always recognized his big smile and signature yachting cap. "Little kids would come up to our table at a restaurant and point: 'Salty Sol!' Salty Sol! Can I have your autograph?' And he would always accommodate them, and be nice to them, no matter that they interrupted our dinner. That's the way he was."

Veteran bay area sportscaster Dick Crippen, who worked at the competition – both WFLA and at WLCY-Channel 10 (the ABC affiliate) – concurred.

On the air, Crippen reflected, "He (Sol) was literally talking to everybody. I think he set a very high standard as far as that presentation went. I think people felt at home with him.

"I knew Sol on and off the screen, and he was a great guy. He often told me he wished he'd hired me, and I took that as a very high compliment. But I knew very well that he'd hired Andy, and he did just fine with Andy."

Andy Hardy, who was Fleischman's assistant in the early days, became WTVT's sports director when the veteran retired in 1974. Although he then had more time to be aboard his beloved boat, Salty Sol couldn't stay away from the station. He continued to do "Where Am I?' until 1984, when he hung up his cap for good.

Andy Hardy

"Andy may have been 18 or 20 when he started with Dad, and he looked like he was 15 or 16," recalled Sol Fleischman Jr. "Andy was wonderful. He allowed Dad not to work so hard. Andy would go out and bird-dog stories and interview sports celebrities. He was a terrific assistant to my dad, and then went to take over after he left."

Quick-witted Pennsylvanian Andy Hardy always contended he'd been named for the character in those old Mickey Rooney movies. Prior to joining WTVT in 1962, he'd played on a championship Army baseball team. He and Salty Sol, 20 years Hardy's senior, were a perfect match – "almost like father-and-son," said Sol Jr.

"Andy," remembered Mike Clark, who worked in the station's production department and now operates Big13.com, a website devoted to WTVT history, "was brilliant and very, very funny. Like Sol, he was always joking and laughing with the crew. And he had an encyclopedic mind for sports. When you're reading off these stats, and you're looking at copy and watching the monitor, you have to have an overall knowledge of what's going on and be able to articulate it."

"When we were off the air, we were competitive but friends," offered Dick Crippen, who like Hardy exuded a boyish excitement on the air. "But on the air, we were out to get the ratings. It was a good game."

Still, Crippen remembered, when the competitors were at a high school football game, for example, and one ran out of film for his camera (in the days before video was ubiquitous), the other would gladly pull an extra reel out of his bag and hand it over. They did it out of respect.

Crippen also thinks he and Hardy were pioneers in local TV – they did more than just "rip and read" stats and wire copy. They actually went to the events themselves and talked to folks. "We both had big followings on Friday night," he said.

"It was a battle, but I think we brought in a more modern take on the sports. Not to say Sol and the other sports guys weren't getting out! But when Andy and I got in there, both of us were fighting a little bit harder for ratings. So we were getting out a lot, and I think that made the difference."

Hardy was also adept at live in-studio bantering with the cartoonish wrestlers from Gordon Solie's *World Champion Wrestling From Florida*, for which WTVT provided production.

Mary Ellen and her sidekick, Poopdeck.

"Andy had offers from other stations, but I think the Tampa Bay area was very interesting to him, because all the baseball teams did their spring training there," Clark explained. "And there were plenty of opportunities to interview the top people in sports."

He was WTVT's sports director for 22 years, resigning for health reasons in 1996, not long after Fox took the station over.

Paul Reynolds & Shock Armstrong

One of Andy Hardy's most memorable roles on Big 13 was as the "dinner companion" of Manuel Beiro, the real-life owner of Valencia Garden, a Spanish restaurant just down Tampa's Grand Central (later Kennedy) Boulevard from WTVT headquarters.

Every Friday night, just after the 11 p.m.

Paul Reynolds by day...

news, Hardy and Beiro – live in the studio – would offer a Sangria toast ("Salud and happy days") and proceed to talk about whatever freshly-prepared specialties the restauranteur had brought with him that night. It was a paid commercial spot.

Each toast ended with a number, i.e. "Salud and happy days No. 1,165," and a persistent bay area rumor was that Beiro was calling out the winning numbers in a popular-but-illicit Cuban lottery game called bolita. In truth, he was announcing, out of sequence, how many commercials he'd done at WTVT since the late 1950s. It was an inside joke, although the legend persists, to this day, about the bolita numbers.

When they were done, Hardy would introduce *Shock Theatre* – the weekly late-night scary movie. And the grateful studio crew would chow down on fresh Spanish food.

It's impossible, though, to talk about Valencia Garden – or *Shock Theatre* – without mentioning Paul Reynolds.

A disc jockey for St. Pete's WTSP radio, Reynolds was hired as WTVT's first "booth announcer," meaning it was his mellifluous voice doing all the announcements, all the commercials ... he even signed the station on the air on Day One, April 1, 1955.

He was a sports reporter and announcer. He hosted a teenage dance party show, and a late-night interview program ... which is where he first encountered new sponsor Manuel Beiro and Valencia Garden.

Reynolds was the "Salud and happy days" guy until 1968, when he left the station, for greener pastures, after a dozen years.

He'd briefly "played" Bozo the Clown on the WTVT's earliest children's segments, and in 1965 the station manager told him he'd be debuting as Shock Armstrong, the "host" of *Shock Theatre,* on Friday nights.

"There wasn't anything that Paul Reynolds couldn't do," explained Clark. "You just plug him in and he goes. And when they told him he was going to be Shock Armstrong, he didn't even blink. A week later, they had the mask, they had the shirt, and he's on the air."

The mask was a cheap, all-purpose Frankenstein number with a zipper up the back – it was too big but Reynolds wore it

... and by night, as "teenage ghoul" Shock Armstrong.

anyway – and his costume was a University of Tampa football jersey (Number 13, of course) with shoulder pads.

Shock was, the station declared, a "teenage ghoul," and he presided over a set made up to look like the bedroom of a messy adolescent.

The films, which stations in those days bought as a syndicated package (this one was literally called *Shock*) included old Universal monster titles and science fiction B-movies from the '50s.

Shock Armstrong slept in a coffin, was devoted to his fuzzy wolfman doll Lamby-Pie, and was tormented by the off-camera screams from his (never-seen) mother. In the first episodes, he merely grunted. But Reynolds, an adept ad-libber, developed a (grouchy) personality for his character. And when Shock began to talk, and complain, and make crummy jokes, he developed a solid following of young fans.

No footage exists from those early, videotaped days (there's no *Good Day*, either, or *Mary Ellen*, and only a few minutes of a black-and-white episode of *Pulse*). Tape was expensive, so each week's show was recorded over when it was time to do the next one.

But Shock Armstrong, at least in memory,

Hugh Smith joined WTVT as a reporter in 1963, and was promoted to news director and anchor in 1968, a position he held for 15 years.

remains.

"There was something about the character that resonated with viewers," Clark said. "He became popular, so much so that when you said 'Channel 13,' that was sometimes the first name they came up with. If they grew up in a certain era."

Shock Theatre continued, without a live host, until 1974 when the CBS network launched its first (failed) attempt at programming against Johnny Carson and the *Tonight Show.*

Hugh Smith

Longtime news director and anchor of *Pulse,* the evening newscast, Hugh Smith's no-nonsense style and stentorian delivery projected an air of authority and confidence. The Midwesterner joined WTVT as a reporter in 1963, and was promoted to news director in 1968, a position he held for 15 years. As such, he managed a staff of 30 people – all while anchoring the news, at noon and again in the evenings, five days a week. And doing his own reporting.

He was, say all who knew him, the consummate news professional.

Weary of the grind, Smith voluntarily stepped down as news director. "I worked for Hugh, and then Hugh worked for me," laughed Ray Blush, who took over the managerial position. "Hugh was one of the best employees I had – he knew what I had to go through as news director, because he had been on that train."

Smith remained in the Top Dog spot, news anchor, until 1991, all the while continuing to report – and write, and film, and edit – stories on his own.

Among the many things he brought to Channel 13, Smith doggedly covered the unsteady politics of the Hillsborough County School Board.

"I thought everybody came out of the TV," said Smith's son Ward. "They all lived in there with Dad – Ernie Lee, John Wayne, Flip Wilson's gotta be in there. But when I went to the station, they weren't there. And the control room was like NASA."

Sometimes, Dad would bring them into the Tampa studios on Saturdays, if he had something to attend to. "Everything was shot on film in those days, and I'd go into the edit rooms," Smith recalled. "All the cut film would be in tubs on the floor.

"Andy Hardy showed me how to put the films into the Moviola, watching all this University of Tampa sports footage – 'if you run it backwards, you can watch the guy running backwards.' I'd stand there for hours just watching a guy throw a football, and catching it backwards.

"I found somebody's stuff that was already on the Moviola, in the editor. And I cut it up and turned it upside down."

Oops. "It must have been somebody's story, ready to go."

And that was it for young Ward's visits to WTVT central command. Today, he is an actor and comedian, and the co-owner (with his sister Karen) of The Off-Central, a playhouse on 1st Avenue South.

Smith does, however, have warm and fuzzy memories of the annual Big 13 Christmas parties, and of accompanying the old man to Media Day at places like Busch Gardens and Walt Disney World, where he was allowed to ride the rides – for free – as much as he wanted.

And he remembers being proud of his father, who was a WTVT fixture – for some, the very voice and face of Big 13 – for 27 years.

"When we would go out, people would come up and say 'Hey Hugh, we saw that

For 40 years, Roy Leep was WTVT's chief meteorologist, and one of the most recognizable (and trusted) television news personalities in the bay area.

story you did on City Hall. You keep those officials honest.' Everybody would say nice things. 'We watch you every night. Keep up the good work.' That was kind of a neat thing."

Mary Ellen

Mary Ellen Colchagoff and her husband left Ohio, and its bitter winters, for St. Petersburg in 1957. She brought along a kinescope of *Fun Farm,* the children's show she'd hosted back home in Toledo, and when the general manager of WTVT saw it, he hired her on the spot to host *Popeye Playhouse* and, later, *Giant Kids Matinee.* With a live parrot called Poopdeck perched on her shoulder, Mary Ellen (her surname, not exactly TV-friendly, was dropped) she introduced cartoons, drew pictures and talked merrily to the 12 to 15 kids comprising her "studio audience."

This was created as direct competition for *Captain Mac's Adventure Trails,* aired live via weak UHF signal from the Million Dollar Pier by WSUN-Channel 38. Like Burl McCarty, who played Captain Mac, Mary Ellen became a local celebrity and made frequent personal appearances in Tampa and St. Petersburg.

By 1962, her popular half-hour had been re-titled *The Mary Ellen Show*. It aired weekday afternoons, sandwiched between a half-hour of shorts and cartoons hosted by space adventurer "3-D Danny" (WTVT staff announcer Ed Scott) and his robot "Ruffnik," and *Pulse,* the evening news program.

Both *3-D Danny* and *The Mary Ellen Show* were televised live, back-to-back, from the same studio.

On his website, Mike Clark wrote: "At one point in the program, Mary Ellen would have the kids look directly into the camera for the 'Magic Eye.' The Magic Eye was actually a special effect created by the switcher in the control room. As the camera panned from one child to the next, the director would use a circle wipe and surround the child's image with the CBS eye.

"When the camera stopped on the 'chosen' child, the circle would vibrate, signifying that this lucky youngster was 'King' or 'Queen' for the day. The child was then adorned with a royal scepter and crown and given a prize, usually a food product from whatever sponsor was on the show that week. How often I envied the lucky youngster who walked away with an arm-sized Tootsie Roll containing several days' worth of treats!"

The Mary Ellen Show was canceled in 1964.

Roy Leep

For 40 years, Roy Leep was WTVT's chief meteorologist. That's not a world record, but it's darn close, and generations of area TV-watchers, from the Big 13 era to the more contemporary days of Fox 13, learned to rely on the soft-spoken Kentuckian for the latest updates and the most accurate forecasts.

"The weather in Central Florida is very interesting for a weatherman," Mike Clark observed. "And he really upped the game for weather reporting on local television." Because of Roy, WTVT became the first television station in Florida to buy and install its own radar station. He helped

design new forecasting technology. He flew in hurricane spotter planes. He was obsessive, and he was thorough.

Paul Dellegatto has been with the WTVT weather department since 1990, before it transitioned into Fox 13. When Leep retired in 1997, he became Chief Meteorologist, a position he's held since. Dellegatto knew he had some big shoes to fill, as Roy Leep, with his measured, studious-but-friendly delivery, was virtually synonymous with Tampa Bay TV.

Reporting anything on television – news, sports or weather – takes a skillful combination of journalistic skills and likeability, along with a smattering of showbiz. "You want the viewer to feel like you're right there in their living room," said Dellegatto. "And Roy had such a great way of talking. I always admired his communication style, which was kind of folksy, yet very smooth. He was a good explainer. The business is all about communication."

Scud the Weather Dog, Leep's own cairn terrier, added the showbiz factor on 1990s broadcasts.

That fact that Leep established himself in the days before apps, computers and cell phones was crucial to his success, according to Dellegatto. "In that era, there was really no place else to go to get weather, except on TV," he said. "People went to a person that they would trust, and have confidence in – and in this market, he was that man.

"And in those 40 years he was able to introduce a lot of technology that people just weren't used to seeing, whether it was radar, satellites … along with a delivery style that was comforting and reassuring and confident, he had a lot of good equipment. And the station had a great reputation. It was a powerhouse station. So a lot of things came together to make him the legend that he was."

Fascinated by the weather since his teenage years, Leep maintained a weather station at his home until his death in 2021. He had been a member of the American Meteorological Society for over 60 years, and was elected a Fellow.

It was, Dellegatto believes, Lee's scientific understanding of hurricanes and the other severe weather that plagues Florida that endeared him to viewers.

"That's really what happens in this business – over time, you go through a number of major storms, and people will be watching. If you give people the proper information, if you deliver it in a way that's not alarming, you will build a big following over time.

"Because people will come to trust you. And I think that was a big reason for his success."

Ernie Lee

When Ernie Lee came to Tampa/St. Pete in 1954, he was already a regional star in the Midwest, making regular appearances on radio (in his native Kentucky) and on fledgling television stations in Cincinnati and Detroit. A singer, guitar player and bandleader born Ernest Eli Cornelison, he'd released a handful of catchy country music singles (both 78s and 45s) on various labels including MGM and RCA. They were regional, not national hits; Lee was a personable, likeable southerner with a smooth baritone voice and a keen sense of humor.

He was invited down by an old friend then working at WSUN, the area's first TV station, and he worked there for four years (*Ernie Lee and the Florida Ranch Boys, The Beach Club with Reba Fox and Ernie Lee* and *Riddle-dee-dee with Ernie Lee*).

Good Day premiered on WTVT April 15, 1958, showcasing Lee with a country band that included the singing husband-and-wife team Herb and Kay Adams, old friends from Ohio, and other musicians he knew from his midwestern days.

Both Herb and Kay take solo turns on the locally-produced album *Ernie Lee's Big 13 – Songs From the 'Good Day' Show*, issued in 1956.

Mike Clark, who worked on the studio crew for most of the 1970s, said Ernie Lee was a presence you could not miss. "I'm not a country music fan myself, but Ernie was so charming and so great I kind of got lured into it," Clark explains. "He turned me around.

"All these on-air people had a really good relationship with the people around them on the crew. With Ernie Lee, if you were just starting or if you had been there a few years, he treated you equally."

Lee stayed with the station until 1991,

Ernie Lee (far right) and the 1950s "Good Day" gang: Charles "Red" Seal, Herb Adams, Kay Adams and Randy Tate.

when declining health forced him to retire. He died less than a year later, after 34 years at WTVT.

Ernie's signoff, every morning, was delivered directly into the camera:

"Put on the coffee pot, Jeanie. I'm comin' home."

On every show, he sang his signature song, which ended with a sweet lyrical lullaby for the glory days of Big 13:

Give me Dixie when night is fallin'
And birds are callin' by moonlit streams
Let me lie there
Live and die there
Give me Dixie, land of my dreams.

When the Tampa Bay Buccaneers debuted in 1975, Dick Crippen was sports director for WLCY-Channel 10. He was the Bucs' official radio announcer for 17 seasons. All images in this chapter from the collection of Dick Crippen.

Dick Crippen, swinging for the fences

espite a resume longer than the tri-oval track at Daytona after 200 laps, the dean of Tampa Bay sportscasting swears his career was a combination of luck, timing and a willingness to try new things. "I always loved sports," Dick Crippen says. "I played some sports but I never intended to go into it. But once I got into it, I just got immersed. And I couldn't have been happier."

Crippen retired in 2021 as Senior Advisor to the Tampa Bay Rays. A combination of community relations, PR, consulting, charity work, voiceover recording and lots of rubber-chicken dinners, it was essentially the same job he signed on for in 1999, he says, only back then his title was Executive Director of Community Development (the "senior" designation, he likes to joke, is merely a reference to his grey hair).

Crippen holds the record for the most contiguous years on local television in West Central Florida. From 1966 to 1981, he was sports director for WLCY-TV, through its transition into present-day WTSP. He jumped ship for WFLA, where he was sports director, and one of the area's most recognized and trusted TV personalities, until the Rays lured him away in 1999. He was inducted into the Sports Club of Tampa Bay's Hall of Fame, and the University of Tampa Athletics Hall of Fame.

He was named Florida Sportscaster of the Year four times by the National Sports-

Crippen's first Tampa Bay TV gig, doing the weather for WFLA-Channel 8. He soon moved to competing WLCY.

casters and Sportswriters Association.

Penny, his wife of more than 50 years, first broached the subject of scaling things back. "She said good gravy, you've done over 50 years in broadcasting, and 21 with the Rays. Don't you think it's about time?" Crippen chuckles.

"I'm retiring, but I'll stay with my charity work, the boards I'm on, and maybe some consulting will come along, I don't know."

The longtime resident of St. Petersburg has the perfect sports broadcasting voice – quick, clear, pointed, a little snarky and always, always in command of whatever subject he happens to be talking about.

"I had the opportunity when I was in television, both at WLCY and WFLA, to go to every Top Ten market in the country," Crippen recalls. "But even though the money was absolutely fantastic, and the perks and all that, it was about the lifestyle. Because of the lifestyle, we decided to stay here. We had two kids, and we just said 'We don't want to raise the kids in the city.'"

Dick Crippen grew up in Tenafly, N.J. just across the Hudson River from the biggest city of them all, New York. At Baltimore's Johns Hopkins University, he studied psychology, then advertising – one of his first jobs was operating the film projectors in the "commercial review" room at J. Walter Thompson in Manhattan.

A part-time saxophone player, he launched a jazz program on WJHU, his college's closed-circuit campus radio station.

But it was while working as a page at NBC's Rockefeller Center headquarters that Crippen's interest in broadcasting began in earnest. In the mornings, his job was to seat audiences for *The Price is Right;* in the early evening, he worked Jack Paar's *Tonight Show.*

During the hours in between, he hung around the national and local radio floors, ingratiating himself and watching how things were done.

In 1960, Crippen transferred to the University of Tampa. "I got off the plane on a beautiful day and wondered, having left snowy midtown Manhattan, where has this been all of my life?" he recalls. "I have never looked back and never left."

With all his "experience" in the Big Apple, he was made program director of WTUN, the campus station. This led to various on-air shifts at WDAE ("The Towering Sound Around the Bay"), then to WFLA-TV as a booth announcer, reciting the call letters at the top of the hour. "It was," Crippen says, "ideal for a guy going to college." In time, he was offered an on-camera gig, as a fill-in weekend weatherman.

His superlative work doing the Saturday-night track announcements at Sunshine Speedway led to announcing the boat races at Lake Maggiore, which boasted the world's fastest course for inboard hydroplanes. He also freelanced whatever miniscule radio jobs came his way. "At this point, I'm adding anything I

Commander Astro (Crippen) with athlete and "Tarzan" film star Johnny Weissmuller.

Crippen with legendary University of Florida coach Steve Spurrier.

can to my resume," he says. "Back then, it was whatever you could do to make it happen."

Television was well past its infancy in the early 1960s, but the Tampa-St. Petersburg market had a lot of catching up to do. There were two VHF stations – WTVT, the local CBS affiliate, on Channel 13 and the NBC-affiliated WFLA, on Channel 8. On the harder-to-tune-in UHF band was city-owned WSUN, broadcasting from the Million Dollar Pier. WSUN carried most of the national programming from ABC, the red-headed stepchild of TV networks.

Everything changed in 1965 when the owners of WLCY, the top AM station in the market, applied for and were granted a license for a new television station. WLCY-TV had a stronger signal than WSUN, and the ABC affiliation was also transferred. The new arrival was designated Channel 10 on the VHF dial.

Dick Crippen was hired as WLCY's first weatherman.

"The morning guy on WLCY radio was a guy named Don Jones," Crippen recalls. "In 1965, which is when the TV went on the air, Don was coming down to the studios on Central Avenue and doing a kids' show called *Submarine 10*. Unfortunately,

Don was killed in a motorcycle accident later that year. They wanted a kids' show on. And they said to me 'How about you do a kids' show?' Space was big at that time, so they decided I'm Commander Astro, and there I was."

Commander Astro was the host of *Space Station 10*, which broadcast old Roger Ramjet cartoons and early TV serials like *Flash Gordon*. "We didn't really have any script – I'd just get in there and start doing this show, and guys from the radio would all of a sudden show up. They would come in and we'd do a bit. All adlib and just a lot of fun for everybody that was involved."

He was tapped to make personal appearances in costume, meeting his young audience and spreading goodwill for the fledgling Channel 10.

"It was quite an experience, and it was also good training for me as far as adlib was concerned," Crippen says.

A year into the station's existence, sports director Vince Malloy announced his departure to enter local politics. Crippen was offered the job, which came with a five-dollar-a-week raise. He and WLCY bookkeeper Penny Mosher had been dating for a while by then, and the extra money sounded good to him. So he took it. He and Penny married that same year, 1966.

As the third-place station in a market of three, WLCY initially had no muscles to flex. WTVT sports director "Salty" Sol Fleischman and WFLA's Guy Bagli and Milt Spencer were well-established by the time Crippen entered the fray.

"It took some work to get that station recognized," Crippen remembers. "There were times when, honestly, I wasn't invited to the same press conferences, because they didn't even recognize the station. But I constantly worked at it. I did a lot of charity work to just get the name out there and promote the station. And eventually it turned around and I got included in everything."

Tampa Bay had no professional sports teams in those days. "It was 'dig for stories,' Crippen says. "A lot of high school sports. I kind of got my signature out of the high school sports, because I really paid attention to them. I started a Friday night show on Channel 10. I'd send a camera out to the game, and they'd shoot maybe the first half. They'd come back to the station, process the film, edit it real fast, and then we'd have the two coaches come in and sit down with me on the show at night. And talk about the game."

His competitors, he explains, "did the scores, but I took it a step further by actually putting the coaches on the air every

Crippen with Major League Baseball icon Wade Boggs.

Friday night. And that drew a pretty big audience.

"There was one point in my career where I just rode around on a Saturday with my camera guy, and we'd see people playing softball in a park, and we'd stop and do a piece on them – who are they? Well, what happens when you do that is all of those guys who we did the story on are going to tune in. And then they'd tell all the people they know, so they would tune in.

"During those early times, I really had to search for sports."

His station manager from WTUN, Gordon Solie, became the voice of the popular Championship Wrestling From Florida, which taped every week in Tampa and provided fodder for local sportscasts. Crippen announced Tampa Bay Rowdies home games from Tampa Stadium, and continued to freelance with Unlimited Hydroplane, Offshore Power Boat and Drag Boat television shows.

The 1975 arrival of the Tampa Bay Buccaneers was a game-changer. "I've always maintained that when the Buccaneers came in, this area became recognized," Crippen says. "Because there's only a limited number of NFL teams, and this area had one of them."

Crippen, at the time, was announcing weekend NASCAR races from Daytona and Talladega. But his hometown having its own NFL team was too important; he left the Motor Racing Network to do play-by-play and color for the Bucs' first two years; he was the team's official radio announcer for 15 more.

In 1978, WLCY-TV was purchased, and re-assigned the call letters WTSP; Crippen remained as director of sports – and the station's most-recognized air personality – for three years.

With no "non-compete" clause in his contract with the ABC station, Crippen was free to accept a generous offer from rival WFLA.

"You're at a point in life where you're looking forward," he says. "Channel 8 had three or four people in the sports department; I had two, myself and one guy. And they had a fulltime camera assigned to sports – I had to beg and borrow from the news department. Salary entered into it also.

"It was a step up, because no matter what, 8 and 13 were always the predominant stations. Channel 10 was working up, and it was getting bigger and bigger. But it was hard for people to pick up until cable came in. Cable helped out tremendously on that."

Crippen served as WFLA's sports director until 1999 with century's end. By then, he was the most respected name in bay area sportscasting. An early champion of the Tampa Bay Rays, he covered every aspect of Major League Baseball in the area, from the earliest site negotiations to the last inning of the last game of the 20th century. He covered the debut of the Tampa Bay Lightning in 1992.

His final WFLA broadcast was on New Year's Eve, 1999, a Friday. The following Monday, he moved into the Rays front office as Executive Director of Community Development.

"I was very honored to have that title," Crippen says, "because Don Zimmer had an identical title. He did the baseball side, I was more on the business side. Actually, what it enabled me to do was to be available to any of the departments – so I was able to help out sales, tickets, community relations ... in other words I didn't really have a specific launch pad. I was able to move around the company and get involved in a lot of different things."

Crippen's list of charity and public service work is staggering, almost as long as his broadcast sports C.V. Among those for whom he has labored tirelessly: Johns Hopkins All Children's Hospital, Suncoast Ronald McDonald Houses, the Chi Chi Rodriguez Foundation, PARC, St. Petersburg YMCA, Blossom School and the Salvation Army. He is on the advisory board of Charity Works, which unites business interests with philanthropic efforts.

He helped launch the Rays of Hope Foundation, which became the Rays Baseball Foundation.

Organization president Brian Auld praised Crippen in a statement. "In his time with the Rays, he has done anything and everything asked of him – promoting our community outreach efforts, keeping our fans informed, and even honing his comedic skills as a regular contributor to Raysvision.

"Perhaps most influentially, he has also served as a friend and mentor to so many of us within the organization. The Rays and the region are better for having had Dick Crippen in our lives."

Crippen was WFLA's sports director from 1981 until 1999. WFLA-TV.

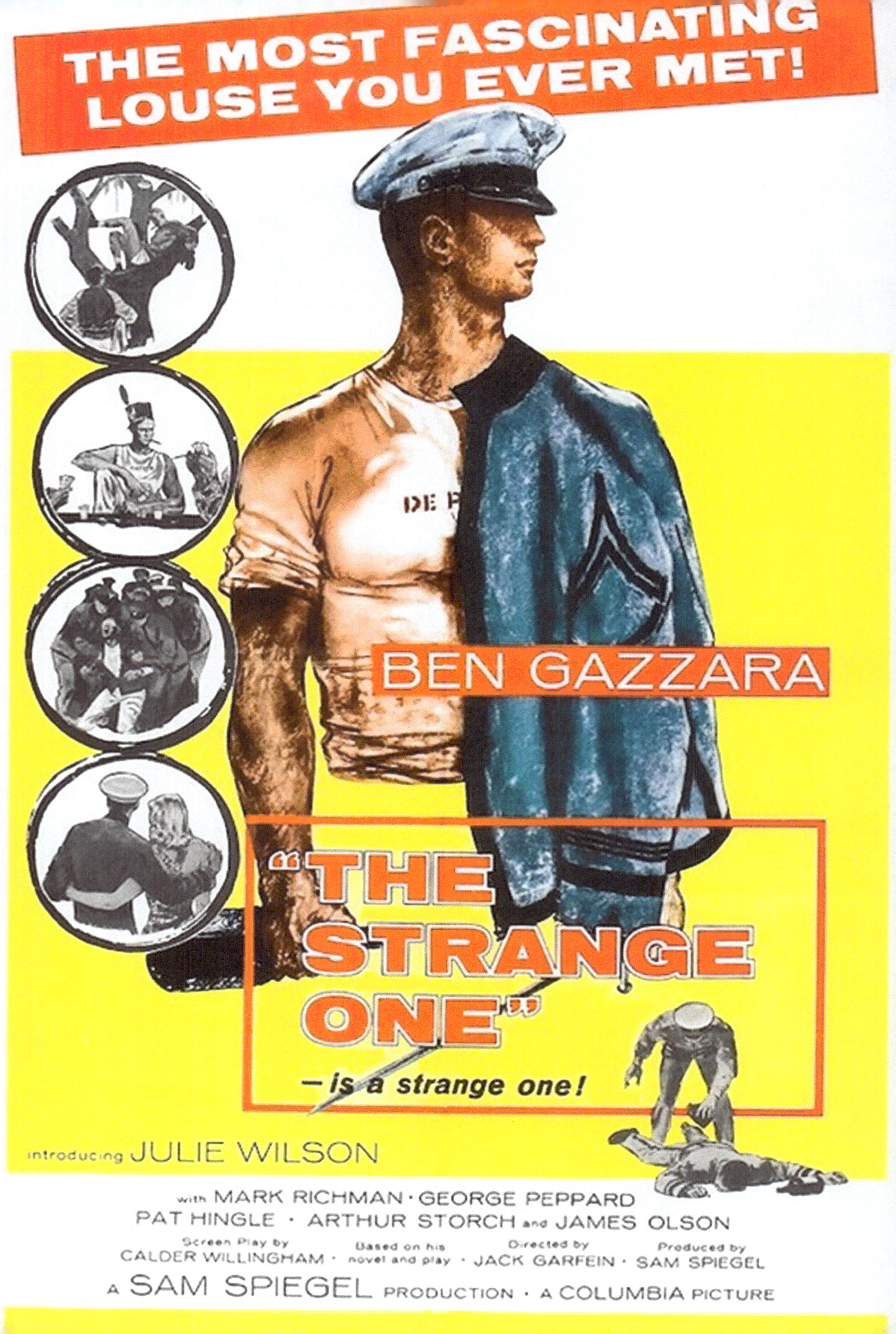
THE MOST FASCINATING
LOUSE YOU EVER MET!
DE P
BEN GAZZARA
"THE
STRANGE
ONE"
–is a strange one!
introducing JULIE WILSON
with MARK RICHMAN · GEORGE PEPPARD
PAT HINGLE · ARTHUR STORCH and JAMES OLSON
Screen Play by CALDER WILLINGHAM · Based on his novel and play · Directed by JACK GARFEIN · Produced by SAM SPIEGEL
A SAM SPIEGEL PRODUCTION · A COLUMBIA PICTURE

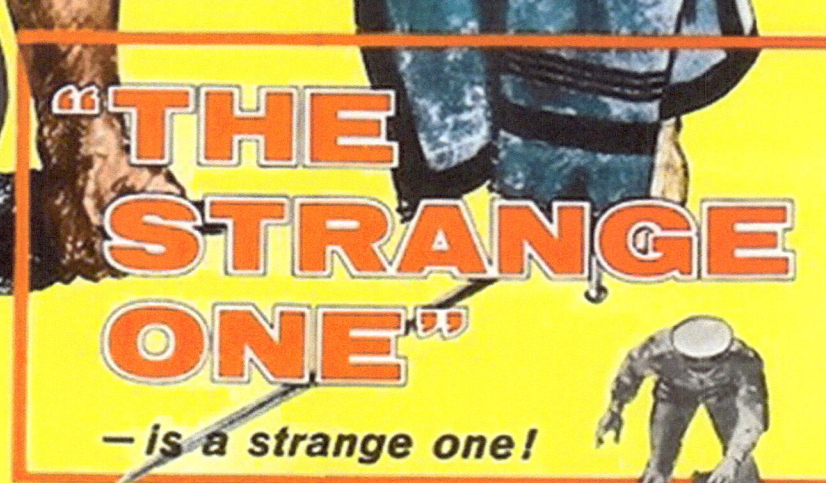

Ben Gazzara, left, and the cadets outside Gulfport's Stetson College. Screengrab. All images in this chapter. Columbia Pictures.

Making a 'Strange' movie in Gulfport

ulfport's stately Stetson University College of Law was a product of the 1920s Florida Land Boom. Developer I.M. "Handsome Jack" Taylor put up the Mediterranean Revival-style compound in the newly-created Pasadena Estates subdivision, cleverly naming his creation Hotel Rolyat – his surname spelled backwards.

According to history, Babe Ruth signed his 1932 contract with the New York Yankees in the hotel lounge.

That same year, the Rolyat was sold to the Florida Military Academy, which operated there until 1953, when the property was again sold, this time to DeLand's Stetson University to expand its law school into a larger metropolitan area.

When Hollywood producer Sam Spiegel (*The African Queen, On the Waterfront*) needed an authentic southern military academy (or at least something that could pass for one) for his cinematic adaptation of Calder Willingham's play *End As a Man*, his location people brought Stetson to his attention.

Willingham had adapted the play from his novel, loosely based on his own experiences at The Citadel, South Carolina's legendary military college. The play, starring newcomer Ben Gazzara and directed by Jack Garfein, had been a Broadway hit, and Spiegel – who was concurrently filming *The Bridge on the River Kwai* in Ceylon – arranged to shoot *End As a Man* in Florida's hottest month, July. The year was 1956.

Interiors would be lensed at a soundstage in Winter Park, near Orlando, while Stetson College of Law would pass for the story's fictional academy for the all-important outdoor scenes of cadets drilling and marching in the squinting sun, and for the actors as they moved from one building to the other.

Spiegel brought his A-team, including Academy Award-winning Director of Photography Burnett Guffey (*From Here to Eternity*), and Art Director Joe Wright (*The Man With the Golden Arm*).

Like those films, *End As a Man* was to be a gritty, realistic portrait of something people in polite society didn't talk about. The central character, cadet Jocko DeParis, is a sadistic upperclassman who bullies and humiliates his fellow students mercilessly.

Central to the plot is an incident in which Jocko (played by Gazzara) intimidates a couple of terrified freshmen into helping him get someone he simply doesn't like – the son of an officer at the school – expelled for drinking on campus.

Gazarra, director Garfein and several other lead actors were from Lee Strasberg's

Gazzara and Arthur Storch.

Gazzara and Paul Reynolds.

Actors Studio in New York; they were all imported directly from the Broadway production of *End As a Man*.

In June, the *St. Petersburg Times* announced that Spiegel and company were seeking locals to work as extras on the July 2-7 shoot:

The scenes here will require the services of 190 young men between the ages of 18 and 22 or, if big enough, boys of 16 or 17. They prefer men who have had military academy, National Guard or ROTC training.

Extras, who trained for a week prior to filming under the tutelage of a retired Army colonel imported from Fort Lauderdale, were paid $3 per hour and given a box lunch.

A 75-millimeter Civil War-era cannon was rented from a St. Petersburg homeowner, and placed on the Stetson lawn during the drill sequences – just another extra, to give the film a touch of authenticity. It was not fired.

St. Petersburg's Hugh Doebrick, who

The source material for "A Strange One" was Calder Willingham's play "End As a Man," which had starred Gazzara, and others from the film cast, on Broadway.

was at that time a cadet at The Citadel, served as Garfein's technical advisor, tweaking the actors' motions as they impersonated military students.

Garfein was accompanied by his wife, actress Carroll (*Baby Doll*) Baker, who had lived for a time in St. Petersburg during her teenage years.

Columbia Pictures' on-set publicity flack, George Nelson, told the *Tampa Tribune* that some changes were made to Willingham's story. "Many of the extremely morbid aspects of the novel, a best-seller of several years ago, have been taken out of the movie," the paper reported.

Most significantly, the play's homoerotic subplot was almost completely excised; in the film, it is implied that DeParis' seething hatred of freshman cadet Simmons (played onstage and onscreen by Arthur Storch) stems from the younger man's effeminate nature.

The movie adds a scene in which DeParis "forces" Simmons to "go on a date" with a local floozy, played by Julie Wilson (also making her film debut).

It's conceivable, too, that Spiegel and Garfein had this tacked on simply to add a woman to the otherwise all-male cast, for broader box office appeal.

Then there's Perrin, another young cadet targeted by DeParis. As played in the movie by Paul E. Richards, he is doe-eyed, soft-spoken and "artistic," and therefore stereotypically gay. He is infatuated with the older student, who treats him reprehensibly.

In the movie, Perrin, who knows what DeParis has done, blackmails him into ... we never find out what. They have an uneasy interaction, during which Perrin reads his poetry aloud ("I have the fire of genius in me") while DeParis fumes and waves his sword around. It's a purposely uncomfortable scene, and typical of drama films of the era, its implication is left to the viewer.

In its June 5, 1957 review of the finished picture, the Village Voice bemoaned the excising, at the censor's request, of three minutes of "vivid moments, especially those focusing on the homosexuality – scenes which truly earned excitement and applause when the picture was previewed at the Sheridan a few months ago."

(It is unclear whether the poetry scene, which is intact in the film in its DVD version, was the same material excised from that first theatrical release.)

A significant book and stage subplot concerning De Paris' father, a major contributor to school coffers, was also removed for the film. And the ending was completely changed.

The phrase "end as a man" never appears, so it may well have seemed logical for Spiegel to change the title. Before release, the film's name was changed to The Strange One – another phrase that

no one in the cast utters.

Was it because DeParis was "strange"? Or the things depicted were "not right"?

Or that the movie was, simply, hard to explain?

The PR wizards handling Columbia's marketing campaign didn't seem to know, either. The movie's trailer begins with these words: The Strange One is a strange one.

Writing in the New York Times, Bosley Crowther said that The Strange One delivered a diluted version of the central point of both the novel and the play, "the fact that brutalization and corruption of young men were ironically fostered and shielded by the 'code of honor' in exis-

A Columbia Pictures publicity photo, showing Gazzara and the other "cadets" drilling at Stetson.

tence at a Southern military school."

Instead, the critic complained, "Mr. Garfein in his direction has engendered an atmosphere of mystery and malevolence in the barracks that is appropriate to a minor horror tale."

Over the decades the film achieved a semi-legendary status as a film noir, for its black and white photography and stark subject matter.

It's never been considered a "classic," even a minor one.

In an interview conducted for the 2009 DVD release, Gazzara explained that the film might have tanked because Columbia put all its marketing muscle into Spiegel's other 1957 movie, *The Bridge on the River Kwai.*

Spiegel, the actor said, had attempted to fire director Garfein from *The Strange One*, but let it go at the last minute. Their friendship never recovered, and Garfein's filmmaking career ended shortly thereafter.

"When the picture was over, and cut and scored, Sam was finished," explained Gazzara. "He never promoted it. There was no money for PR. It was thrown out there; there was no money for distribution. He just killed it. Long memory."

JOSEPH FIENNES
RAY LIOTTA
GRETCHEN MOL

A FILM BY PAUL SCHRADER

FOREVER MINE

Some desires are too dangerous to resist.

"One of the Best American Movies of the Year."
- Salon.com

Selena Gomez, Vanessa Hudgens and the other bank-robbing "Spring Breakers" roar past the Beach Theatre on Corey Avenue. A24.

Rolling: Still more movies on location

Ray Liotta took the red-eye from Los Angeles to Tampa on March 7, 1999, and when he stumbled off the plane, around 4 a.m., the actor was detained by airport police.

Flight attendants had accused the *GoodFellas* star of becoming verbally abusive when they declined to serve him more wine. The legal complaint included the phrase "drunk and belligerent."

Liotta was on his way to St. Pete Beach to shoot *Forever Mine*, a thriller about an adulterous affair and a vengeful spouse. Considering the film's hostile reviews, and its subsequent reputation as the first real stinker of the new millennium, perhaps Liotta, who had obviously read the script, was merely pounding drinks to steel himself for what was to come.

"So listless and numbing we need not wonder why it went directly to cable," wrote the *New Yorker*.

Writer/director Paul (*American Gigolo*) Schrader and company spent a month camped at the Don CeSar making *Forever Mine,* in which new bride Ella Brice (Gretchen Mol) has a steamy romance with handsome cabana tender Alan Ripley, a.k.a. underachieving Manuel Esquema (British actor Joseph Fiennes, employing a cheesy Latin accent).

Sample dialogue, spoken under a pink beach umbrella:

Ella: I'm married. I'm here six more days.

Manuel/Alan: And I'm a towel boy. Isn't it

March 21, 2012. Hundreds of local extras "party" at the Coral Reef Beach Resort to make "Spring Breakers" seem real. Tampa Bay Times/Zuma Press.

perfect?

(They kiss.)

Considering Fiennes was just coming off the hit *Shakespeare in Love,* he must have thought *Forever Mine,* which included several soft-focus sex scenes, would constitute the next rung in his ladder of hot-hunk success.

Wrong!

Forever Mine is a by-the-numbers melodrama, part sexy romp and part violent psychodrama (that'd be the segments with Liotta, playing histrionic hubby Mark Brice). And except for several long, loving shots of the beach, and the pink Don CeSar architecture, it could have been made anywhere. And just as forgotten.

Liotta's "drunk and belligerent" case was dismissed.

Beauties and the beach

The critics were somewhat kinder to *Spring Breakers,* the next big-budget Hollywood movie to come to St. Pete Beach. Writer/director Harmony Korine's drama about four bikini-wearing college girls on the loose during a particularly hedonistic Spring Break plays like a cross between

Girls Gone Wild and *Reservoir Dogs*.

No wonder Quentin Tarantino declared *Spring Breakers* his favorite movie of 2013.

James Franco plays cornrowed rapper-slash-drug dealer Alien, who takes the young ladies under his "wing" and leads them into a life of violent crime.

The film's marketing campaign was centered entirely on the four nearly-naked and apparently brain-dead women (played by former Disney stars Vanessa Hudgens and Selena Gomez, along with Ashley Benson and Rachel Korine, the director's wife).

On March 13, 2012, the film company spent three hours on Corey Avenue, as the quartet of celebrity nubiles rode scooters up and down, back and again, to the cheers of extras in T-shirts and swimsuits, toasting the "hottie biker gang" with cans, bottles and open containers of (fake) beer.

On March 21, the stars and 500 local extras gathered in and around the pool at the Coral Reef Beach Resort for the movie's biggest, loudest and most Bacchanalian scene. They danced, they screamed, they raised their ever-present beverages in the air.

St. Petersburg High student Angela Skane

The steamy drama "Forever Mine," With Gretchen Mol and Joseph Fiennes pitching woo outside the Don CeSar. J&M Entertainment.

worked as an extra that day, and reported for the *Tampa Bay Times*. Her story began: "'Are any of you comfortable with making out with another girl?' was not something I expected to hear at 10 in the morning."

The extras were not compensated, although girls who were willing to remove their tops and lewdly gyrate for the cameras were paid $150, Skane wrote.

Along with its many scenes of titillation, public drunkenness and drug use, *Spring Breakers* showed the world an image of St. Pete Beach – yes, it's called that in the movie – that doesn't actually exist. Certainly not as a ground zero for anything-goes spring breakers.

Twitter, Instagram and the other social media outlets were all gaga, however, when Gomez, the film's breakout star, turned up unexpectedly at stores or restaurants, sometimes in the company of her boyfriend, Justin Bieber. The actress happily signed autographs and posed for photos.

Additional scenes were filmed at the Gulfport Police Department, at the Sunshine Skyway Bridge and on the Redington Long Pier. The company left town before March turned to April.

Cross-country comedy

Considerably more extras were needed for the comedy *Coupe de Ville*, which required several scenes set at a Florida dog racing track. Derby Lane fit the bill, although it was closed for the season when the filmmakers came calling in June, 1989.

So they paid extra (a lot extra) dough to have employees – and dogs – all dressed for business and ready to go when actors Patrick Dempsey and Daniel Stern turned up to "place a bet." In the movie, they (along with Arye Gross) play estranged brothers who bond during a road trip across country in a powder-blue Cadillac Coupe de Ville.

The call went out for 3,000 extras to dress in "late '50s, early '60s conservative night wear" for two evenings of providing human background. Approximately 2,000 arrived on the first night. After sitting out a downpour, cast, crew and extras got to work.

The Derby Lane sequences were finished the following night.

Coupe de Ville turned its attention to the Snell Isle Bridge, where Dempsey, Gross and Stern shot another scene (their prized car is threatened by tough guys wielding baseball bats).

From left Daniel Stern, Arye Gross and Patrick Dempsey on the Snell Isle Bridge in the road comedy "Coup de Ville." Screengrab/Universal.

The production company donated $2,000 to the Property Owners Association beautification project, as a way of apologizing for holding up traffic during the two days it took to film the brief sequence.

The six-day shoot wrapped on June 28, as Stern and Dempsey were filmed walking into Center Jewelers on 1st Avenue North. Movies are generally shot out of sequence, so this scene was to come before the Derby Lane material in the finished film.

"*Coupe de Ville*," Roger Ebert said in his review, "is composed of so many formulas that they must have a template for it in screenwriting school."

Game, set, match

The low-budget tennis drama *The Break* borrowed a well-worn sports-movie formula (from *Rocky* to *The Karate Kid* to *The Mighty Ducks* to *Happy Gilmore*, even): The underdog beats the odds, and the underhanded machinations of an arrogant champion, to WIN THE BIG GAME!

This 1995 non-starter was written and produced by former child actor Vincent Van Patten, son of *Eight is Enough* star Dick Van Patten. He cast himself as the bitter, washed-up tennis pro who coaches a hopeless young upstart (Ben Jorgensen) all the way to the top.

The climactic tournament scene was lensed at the Vinoy Resort in St. Petersburg over several days in September 1993.

Actors Van Patten, Jorgensen and Rae Dawn Chong were there to work, along with several hundred extras. And seated in the "grandstands" was Martin Sheen, who was playing the Jorgensen character's wealthy, distant dad. He was filmed watching the "match." When his son emerged triumphant, dad embraced him and gave a short, moving speech.

The Break was clearly a time-killing "paycheck movie" for Sheen, still six years away from his career revival on *The West Wing*.

In November, a mini-scandal erupted when hundreds of St. Pete and Orlando crew members and craftsmen complained that they had not been paid for their work on the $2.75 million movie. "It was a miscalculation," producer Van Patten told *Times* film writer Steve Persall. "To be quite honest, at the end of the film we found out we ran out of money."

At Jack Russell Stadium, Clearwater, May 1972: Robert De Niro (second from right) in the baseball drama "Bang the Drum Slowly." Screengrab/Paramount.

Van Patten then reassured the cheated workers that the checks were, in fact, in the mail.

Once the financial mess was cleaned up, the film failed to find a distributor, and was released directly to video in 1996.

Catching up

One of the most beloved sports movies of all time, 1973's *Bang the Drum Slowly*, has a Pinellas County connection.

Numerous scenes in the film, Robert De Niro's first as an above-the-title star, were shot in Clearwater in 1972.

Based on the novel by Mark Harris, *Bang the Drum Slowly* is the story of the New York Mammoths, a major league baseball team, and the tensile friendship between star pitcher Henry Wiggen and his best pal, catcher Bruce Pearson.

No one on the team – including coach Vincent Gardenia, a real scenery-chewer – understands why Henry is so devoted to Bruce, who is considered something of a half-wit, and one of the lesser Mammoths. At least one player wonders out loud if they're "fairies."

The audience is let into the secret early – Bruce is dying of Hodgkin's Lymphoma, and Henry is simply trying to do right by his friend.

One of the classic sports-movie tearjerkers, *Bang the Drum Slowly* arrived on the heels of the TV film *Brian's Song*, which featured a similar storyline (albeit set in the world of football).

Members of the cast were filmed at Morton Plant Hospital and Sylvan Abbey Memorial Park.

Although most of the baseball footage was shot at Yankee Stadium and Shea Stadium, Clearwater's Jack Russell Stadium stood in for the Mammoths' Spring Training home.

Moriarty, De Niro and actress Ann Wedgeworth were filmed at a table inside the Hourglass Lounge, inside the Fort Harrison Hotel. De Niro and Wedgeworth took a

In "The Break": At the Vinoy with scrappy tennis player Ben Jorgensen, and Martin Sheen as his disapproving dad. Screengrab/TriMark.

turn around the dance floor.

Times writer Mary O. McKey chronicled her day working as an extra in this scene, and reported that others scenes had been shot on the hotel roof, by the pool, the Cloud Room, the Skyline Room and additional in-house locations.

"Then came the final blows to our egos," McKey wrote, quoting a production assistant: "Just hold the cigarette in your mouth and pretend like you're smoking. You're all so much out of focus in the background that you can't tell the difference anyway."

Wedgeworth, who was at that time appearing on the soap opera *Somerset,* was the only "name" actor participating in the Hourglass Lounge sequence. Moriarty would make his name many years later as Ben Stone, the pre-Sam Waterston assistant district attorney on *Law & Order.*

And De Niro, then just 28 years old, was still a couple of movies away from becoming ROBERT DE NIRO.

His next three, made in quick succession, were *Mean Streets, The Godfather Part II* and *Taxi Driver.*

Winter, whose dramatic story of rescue, hope and courage inspired millions around the world. Clearwater Marine Aquarium.

A film crew from Alcon Entertainment shot the first "Dolphin Tale" in Clearwater in 2010. From the collection of David Yates.

Warm Winters: The 'Dolphin Tale' movies

he story of Winter, the young bottlenose dolphin rescued on the east coast of Florida and brought back to life at the Clearwater Marine Aquarium, resonated around the world. After she lost her tail flukes from entanglement in a crab trap line, the animal was fitted with a custom-made prosthesis, and trained to swim with it.

Winter was saved by a dedicated team of marine biologists, scientists and volunteers.

And the Clearwater Marine Aquarium was itself saved by Winter. Before her arrival in December 2005, attendance at the somewhat ramshackle rescue and rehab center was around 76,000 annually.

Six years later, after the worldwide release of the family film *Dolphin Tale*, CMA was welcoming 800,000 visitors per year.

The Clearwater Marine Aquarium, ramshackle no more, is a global tourist destination.

When David Yates signed on as the facility's CEO in early 2006, he was brought over to the main rehab pool where Winter, barely four months old, was struggling to swim with a rotting tail, and was barely eating. "The whole industry said, she won't survive," Yates recalled. "We were advised to euthanize her."

Indeed, the survival rate for stranded baby dolphins was low – if a marine mammal has beached, that's almost always a sign of impending death.

Winter, however, hung on. And by the fall, Yates, who had run the Ironman Triathlon organization for 11 years and had produced numerous TV specials (winning

Nathan Gamble was 12 years old when he signed on to play Sawyer. Screengrab/Alcon Entertainment.

three Sports Emmys in the process), saw a marketing opportunity.

"The Ironman brand is very like the Winter brand," he explained. "It's about courage, perseverance, never giving up. I thought 'I've got the same story here that I had 10 years ago – I'm going to pitch this the same way.'"

He chronicled Winter's rehabilitation by CMA veterinarians and staff in a series of video mini-documentaries. Over time, these came to include prosthetist Kevin Carroll's introduction of a plastic-and-rubber tail that fit snugly over the dolphin's tail stump.

Yates and CMA dolphin handlers appeared on national TV. Winter's story was picked up by the news wires.

In 2009, Scholastic Press published *Winter's Tail: How One Little Dolphin Learned to Swim Again*, a book for young readers.

The book caught the eye of Los Angeles-based Alcon Entertainment, producers of *The Blind Side*, *Sisterhood of the Traveling Pants* and *Dude, Where's My Car?*

From the start, all involved agreed the movie would balance "feel-good" with the serious part of the story, keeping the science – along with the selfless volunteer spirit – front and center.

Dolphins in captivity at CMA are there because they can't be released back into the wild, for medical reasons. They are not there to perform "tricks" on command.

"And it had to be filmed here, because Winter was here," Yates recalled. "We couldn't stop our animal care work.

"And we're not going to have Winter do stuff she can't do. We're not going to stress her out.

"So a lot of planning went into it: Here's what Winter does; how can we work these into the film?

"We realized that to film properly, we couldn't allow our guests to come in. And attendance wasn't near what it is now. We closed down for 65 days, give or take, and Alcon paid our lost revenue.

"But it was a challenge. We had to tell the hotels, don't send people."

"There was never any question that we'd use the real dolphin," executive producer Robert Engleman explained in the *Orlando Sentinel*. "Winter has this incredible personality, and she's unique. Not having a tail, she moves differently from other dolphins. You can't fake that. No other dolphin could be her double."

Karen Jantzen and Noam Dromi wrote the script for *Dolphin Tale,* wrapping the core of Winter's story into a tidy tale about a shy young boy who bonds with the injured dolphin in her CMA tank, and becomes a key member of Winter's human "family."

Production began in September 2010, with actor Charles Martin Smith (*American Graffiti, Never Cry Wolf, The Untouchables*) in the director's chair.

Smith, whose work as director included the well-received family film *Air Bud*, said of *Dolphin Tale*: "I think people talk down to kids too much. I think kids' movies can be great and carry the weight and pathos of an adult drama. They tend to get short shrift, but the kids are smarter than we give them credit for."

Harry Connick Jr. and Morgan Freeman in "Dolphin Tale." Screengrab/Alcon Entertainment.

Yates was a co-producer on the film, which was shot in 3D. This required particularly large cameras – one reason Alcon built an additional 80,000-gallon tank for Winter on the CMA site. The cameras – and the now 4-year-old dolphin, who'd be "playing" herself – would have plenty of room in which to maneuver.

Characters were combined, eliminated and created from whole cloth to streamline the story that Alcon, Smith and company wanted to tell. Harry Connick Jr. was cast as biologist Clay Haskett, operator of the CMA and Winter's chief caretaker. Morgan Freeman took the role of Dr. Cameron McCarthy, designer of the prosthetic tail. Kris Kristofferson signed on to play Clay's father, and the central role of fictional Sawyer Nelson was played by 12-year-old Seattle actor Nathan Gamble (with Ashley Judd as his widowed mother).

Local extras cheer on Nathan-as-Sawyer in the climactic scene of "Dolphin Tale." Screengrab/Alcon Entertainment.

Now 24, Gamble looks back on his *Dolphin Tale* experience with pride. Still, he recalled, after he was offered the part, there was still a matter of chemistry with his aquatic co-star: Would there be any?

Thus, the litmus test.

"Let's be real: Morgan Freeman is not the star, Harry Connick's not the star … I'm not even the star," Gamble said. "Winter the dolphin is the star. And if Winter the dolphin doesn't like Nathan Gamble, who's going to be Sawyer, then Nathan Gamble's not going to be Sawyer."

Alcon flew him to Florida. "They had me hang out with her for a couple days. I was terrified out of my mind. I was 12 years old and I had never seen a dolphin, let alone swam with the most famous dolphin of all time. It was nerve-wracking at first, for sure."

In time, though, all was going swimmingly. "The more time you spend with a person, the more you get to know them," Gamble said. "What they like and what they don't like. It was the same with Winter.

"There were certain things, movements that I would do with her that she really responded well to – and there were certain movements that maybe she didn't like. So I just wouldn't do that."

It didn't hurt, he confessed, that he always had a bucket of fish handy. "But when it comes to that connection, it built up over time. It was treating Winter not like an animal, but like another actor who has their own personality, in a sense."

Principal photography on *Dolphin Tale* lasted 60 days. Some days, Yates said, Winter, or one of the other dolphins, simply refused to cooperate. Rather than force the issue, which would only stress the animals, the filmmakers would use the time to film another scene, using only the human actors. "We did things on her schedule," according to Yates.

"Dolphins are very intelligent animals. We do a thing called enrichment. All the dolphins had very planned days. We had to keep them mentally engaged. Otherwise, they could get sick and die.

"So we made the movie enrichment. And if Winter just didn't want to do something, we'd do something else."

Although there is computer-generated imagery (CGI) in *Dolphin Tale*, it's used sparingly. Similarly, animatronics and lifelike puppets were utilized on occasion (many of Winter's out-of-water closeups, for example, aren't really her).

Nearly all of the water scenes, according to Gamble, feature the real Winter.

Her handlers worked for months acclimating the dolphin to the mechanics of movie-making. "In order to shoot over water, you've got to have a giant crane with the giant camera attached to the end," Gamble explained. "It hovers around the pool. In order to acclimate Winter, they had a foam thing that looked exactly like the crane. And also, they would have random people in the water, holding giant camera-like things, to just get her used to it.

"Because we never wanted to startle her, and never wanted to force her to do anything she did not want to do."

The company shot additional scenes at Clearwater's Long Center pool, Admiral Farragut Academy, the back yard of a private home on Betty Lane in Clearwater, Satinleaf Avenue in Oldsmar, and on a stretch of Honeymoon Island beach, where Gamble-as-Sawyer happens upon (animatronic) baby Winter tangled in nylon ropes.

Released in 2011, *Dolphin Tale* attracted mostly glowing reviews. "The best family

Cozi Zuehlsdorff (playing Hazel), Winter and Nathan Gamble in "Dolphin Tale 2." Warner Bros.

film to come along in a decade," raved the *Dallas Morning News*. At the box office, it nearly tripled its $37 million budget.

Winter's effect on children around the world was profound. Sure, the thousands who flocked to CMA after *Dolphin Tale* (and its 2014 sequel) came, for the most part, to spend a few minutes with the resilient star of their favorite animal movie.

More than that, however, Winter became a role model for kids with disabilities. "The weekend *Dolphin Tale* came out, from Friday noon to Sunday night, we got 10,000 emails," Yates said. "Just two and a half days.

"The vast majority were from moms saying 'I want to tell you how Winter changed my child's life.' These are Make-a-Wish kids. These are kids in hospital beds in England, having brain tumors and going into surgery."

The letters, emails and video messages poured in: "If Winter can do it, I can do it."

Winter and Hope

Late in the afternoon of Dec. 11, 2010, the final day of principal photography, Yates was at home getting ready for the evening's wrap party at Island Way Grill, next door to the Clearwater Marine Aquarium. Cast and crew would gather to celebrate the ending of filming, then go their separate ways.

He received a call from the CMA rescue team. They were heading back to the east coast, in the same general area where Winter had been discovered. Another baby dolphin had beached in distress. That very day.

This became the talk of the wrap party, and as Yates and members of the CMA staff left to meet the arriving truck around midnight, cast and crew began to migrate over, too.

When the new dolphin, who would be nicknamed Hope, arrived, a CMA veterinarian took her from the back of the truck and carried her up the stairs leading to the rehab pool, rather than waiting for the crane normally used for such work.

This would become a scene in *Dolphin Tale 2*, shot – with all the major cast members returning – in 2013 (Connick's character carried little Hope up the stairs).

Director Smith, who wrote the script, made Hope the star of the sequel. In the story, Winter has sunk into depression following the (natural) death of her 40-year-old tankmate.

Hope arrives, a new bond is formed, and there are smiles all around.

"The first one was such a beautiful package, a great story with a beginning, a middle and an end," Connick told *St. Petersburg Times* writer Steve Persall. "Then I read the second script and was absolutely blown away. There's no wonder why every single person in the cast showed up to do it again."

With visitation at an all-time high because of the worldwide success of the first film, it was decided that closing CMA for two full months – to produce *Dolphin Tale 2* – wouldn't be advisable. So a com-

Sisters and movie stars: Hope, left, and Winter. Clearwater Marine Aquarium.

promise was reached – Alcon had the run of the place on weekdays, but the facility would open for visitors on Saturday and Sundays, with no Hollywood types in sight.

Other locations included Fort De Soto Park, Morgan Stanley Tower, Florida Hospital North Pinellas and the sponge docks (both in Tarpon Springs). Island Way Grill was used for a party scene.

The movie took in $57.8 million, significantly less than its predecessor but more than enough to recoup its costs.

According to the Clearwater Marine Aquarium, the two films combined resulted in a $2 billion impact to Pinellas County. In 2020, CMA opened an $80 million expansion, including a new 1.5 million gallon water habitat.

"There's no place in the world you'll find that impacted more kids in the way that CMA did, because of the movies," Yates beamed.

On Nov. 11, 2021, Winter died from what was later discovered to be a condition called an intestinal torsion. Because of her unusual anatomy, and the stress on her body from the prosthetic tail, the 16-year-old animal was vulnerable to certain health conditions.

Yates, who left CMA in 2020, has begun producing films in and around Finellas County, knows he was part of something incredibly special. "Winter's legacy is about CMA and its mission," Yates said. "And it's about changing the lives of kids, which will never go away."

Gamble frequently visits the bay area, and he says he's humbled to be recognized on the street, more than a decade later, as the young boy who bonded with Winter in those movies.

"I know that most actors would love to say that they were a part of it," he said. "Even if I have only a small percentage of what it was, I'm very blessed to say that I was a part of something like that."

LARGER THAN LIFE

Based out of Pensacola during World War I, Lt. Albert Whitted taught seaplane aviation in the US Army aviation corps. Anne Field collection.

The city-owned Albert Whitted Airport, on the St. Pete bayfront. City of St. Petersburg.

Takeoff: The legend of Albert Whitted

The namesake of St. Petersburg's historic bayfront airfield was also the city's first hometown hero.

Born in St. Pete in 1893, James Albert Whitted was the son of Thomas Albert "T.A." Whitted, who'd relocated from Boone, Iowa, by mule train. He married Julia Jeanettie Phillips; her father Zephaniah, a Civil War veteran, was one of the first wave of Long Key homesteaders. Zephaniah Phillips built the first home on Pass-a-Grille and held several patents for mechanical inventions.

T.A. and Julia built a house of their own in Gulfport; James Albert – everyone called him "Al" – was the third son of nine children (four of his siblings died at a very young age). T.A. built the area's first sawmill, built and installed doors and windows, and played double bass in St. Pete's first orchestra.

A gifted mechanic, like his father and grandfather, Albert Whitted (a graduate of St. Petersburg High School) opened a motorcycle repair and sales shop on Central Avenue. While cycle racing in New Haven, Connecticut, he took an interest in aviation, and subsequently learned not only to fly, but to maintain and repair aircraft.

At the outset of World War I, he enlisted in the US Army aviation corps, and was sent to the naval base in Pensacola, where he taught seaplane aviation. In 1918, he was commissioned as a first lieutenant

and made chief instructor in advanced flying. He married Frances Louise Brent, of Pensacola, and until his tragic death five years later, the couple and their two daughters divided their time between homes in that Panhandle town and St. Petersburg.

From the airplane hangar at the Vinoy Basin – where Tony Jannus had launched his over-water passenger service back in 1914 – Whitted began a sight-seeing company, taking passengers over Tampa Bay and the beaches in his seaplane Bluebird. Early accounts say he did it for free, but eventually started charging $10 per "long" flight.

In 1921, Whitted built an experimental seaplane that was lighter and faster than its predecessor. Falcon, as it was named, had an unusual four-bladed propeller and could reach speeds of 100 mph.

A member of the St. Petersburg Civitan Club, Whitted was lauded for successful rescue missions off the coast, and for his "selfless" dedication to public service. His seaplanes, said his longtime friend Bob Smalley, were "always at the call of anyone" who had a civic purpose.

Lieut. Albert Whitted, local aviator, inaugurated his commercial tours here Saturday in flights to Fort Myers and Tampa. Accompanying him to Fort Myers were E.H. Tomlinson, Art Foster and T.R. Fleet. After returning from Tampa (sic), Lieut. Whitted carried Bob Smalley, Rollin Wilkinson and A.F. Bairnsfather to Tampa, where it was made possible for Smalley to deliver a new automobile to Bairnsfather, just 20 minutes after the car had been ordered in St. Petersburg. Bairns-

father is an artist from New York who is spending the winter here.
St. Petersburg Times/Jan. 21, 1923

Despite the fact that they are planning a seven-day tarpon fishing trip that will take them 50 miles down the gulf cost by Tuesday, Chal. Laughner, Fred Ausiobrook and Joe Kerrick plan to come back to St. Petersburg on that day to vote on the county road bonds and mayor's recall. The trio have arranged with Al Whitted to pick them up wherever they are Tuesday morning in his seaplane Falcon, and whisk them back to the Sunshine city, and then take them again to their tarpon grounds.
St. Petersburg Times/June 2, 1923

What is believed to have been the first non-stop flight between St. Petersburg and Pensacola in a commercial sea-

PLANE CLIMBS ABOVE CLOUDS

Whitted Breaks Year's Altitude Record at 7,000 Feet

Climbing to a height of more than 7,000 feet on the return trip from Tampa Tuesday afternoon.

plane was made Sunday by Lieut. Albert Whitted who left here Sunday morning at 4:45 a.m. reaching Pensacola four and a half hours later. On previous flights to Pensacola Whitted stopped off at Cedar Keys for fuel and gas, but Sunday he put enough fuel on board to take him through the entire trip. He will return here about Christmas to resume his commercial flying business.
St. Petersburg Times/July 3, 1923

On Aug. 19, Whitted was flying Falcon over Santa Rosa Sound, off the coast of Pensacola, with four paying passengers aboard, when the propeller (mounted behind the wings and cockpit) loosened and flew into the rear fuselage, severing all control wires.

The plane plunged 200 feet into the Gulf of Mexico. All five people on board were killed instantly.

James Albert Whitted, just 30 years old,

Mac Sennett's Bathing Beauties with Lt. Whitted, circa 1920. Hollywood film producer Sennett sent these women around the country on promotional tours. Anne Field collection.

was buried at St. Michael's cemetery in Pensacola.

St. Petersburg's lone airfield at the time was Piper-Fuller, where Tyrone Square Mall is now (there was also a private landing strip on Weedon Island).

On Oct. 12, 1928, city commission approved construction of an airfield on the southern bayfront. Known as the Cook-Springfield tracks, some reports suggest there was already a primitive airstrip at the site when (re) construction began. Council earmarked $750 to "clean up" Piper-Fuller by fixing runway potholes and mowing down weeds.

The new facility, named for Albert Whitted, opened in the summer of 1929. It boasted several runways, the longest of which was 2,500 feet.

Initially used for commercial flights (National Airlines flew in and out for a decade, starting in the mid '30s), it was utilized for Coast Guard and other military operations during World War II. Since the 1960s, Albert Whitted Airport has served private and charter air businesses. It remains a city-owned property.

"Albert was a mechanical genius," his nephew Eric Whitted said in 1988. "I am convinced that if the Falcon had survived, it would be hanging in the Smithsonian today."

Whitted (left) with passenger on Bluebird, circa 1919. St. Petersburg Museum of History.

Whitted (seated in cockpit) with passengers, the DuBois family, posing with Falcon in 1922. Whitted died in this seaplane Aug. 19, 1923. St. Petersburg Museum of History.

Chicago-born Leonard George DeStoppelaire, a.k.a. Lenny Dee, sold millions of albums of his easy-listening organ music. He lived and worked in St. Petersburg for nearly 50 years. Decca Records.

Dee's album covers were sometimes more interesting than the easy-listening music inside. This photo is from "Mellow-Dee." Decca Records.

The man, the myth, the music: Lenny Dee

He mostly kept rock music at arm's length, but Lenny Dee was St. Petersburg's first – and to date only – real rockstar. During the period of his greatest success, the 1960s through the '80s, Dee was an internationally-renowned entertainer, averaging two albums per year on one of the biggest record labels in the world.

St. Pete, however, was home, and when he wasn't on the road, touring or recording or appearing on some TV show, Lenny Dee was a devoted family man who ran a successful business on the beach.

The business was Lenny Dee's Dolphin Den, a high-end nightclub and restaurant, and its chief product was Lenny Dee himself, for two shows per night. The Den was always packed with people dressed to the nines – it was strictly a ccat-and-tie joint – who paid to catch the floor show.

Dee played the Hammond electric organ, and his act consisted of current easy-listening hits, alongside good old singa-longs like "Toot-Toot Tootsie Goodbye" and "Has Anybody Seen My Gal?" These were presented along with an array of funny hats and accents, and a stream of corny and occasionally off-color jokes, told from his white organ bench beneath a large mirror that gave the audience a view of his hands as they deftly flew across the twin keyboards. He was, in a word, animated.

Perhaps it sounds quaint these days, when entertainment tends to scream for attention from all sides. But in a simpler time, a big St. Pete night on the town meant the dinner theaters, or the ornate Kapok Tree Inn, maybe dancing at the Coliseum ... or a dinner date at Lenny Dee's Dolphin Den.

Dee's daughter Georgia idolized her old man. "He used to draw people from everywhere, because there was no Disney World, no theme parks in Florida," she says. "St. Pete Beach was a destination location for entertainment.

"But if we went, for example, to St. Peter's Cathedral in New York, the organist there recognized him the minute he walked in. People knew him – he'd say his name and they were like 'Oh my gosh, you're Lenny Dee!'"

He was born Leonard George DeStoppelaire, a Chicago kid whose uncle taught him to play the accordion. Following a Navy stint during World War II, he enrolled,

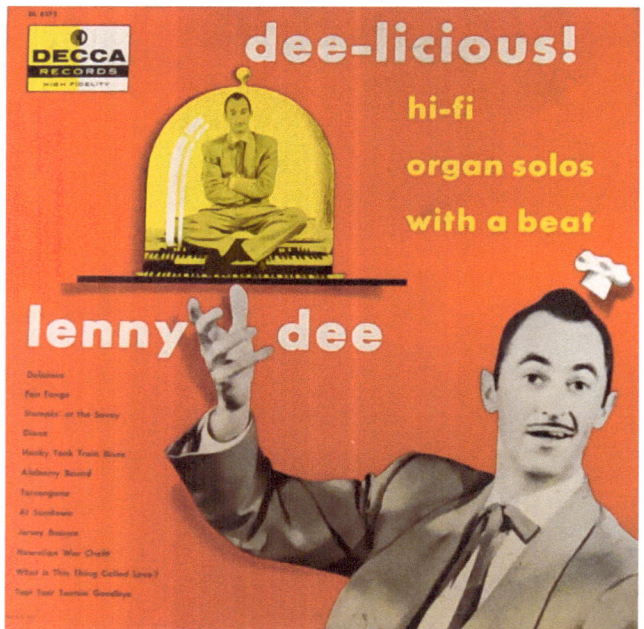

on the G.I. Bill, at the Midwestern Conservatory.

It was there, in 1945, that he discovered the Hammond organ, which used a series of sliding drawbars to create different sounds – and therefore, different combinations of sounds, depending on which bars were pulled or pushed. In an era long before synthesizers, the Hammond could sound like other instruments. He learned the left-handed boogie-woogie. He learned to simultaneously work the bass pedals with his feet.

"After the war, a lot of guys were playing in lounges," Dee recalled years later. "With an organ, you could self-contain yourself. You didn't need other guys."

In 1955 country music star Red Foley caught Dee's one-man-band act at Nashville's Plantation Inn, and recommended him to his label, Decca. With its World War II-era star organist Ethel Smith getting a bit long in the tooth, Decca signed Lenny Dee on the basis of his sprightly instrumental arrangements

Postcard from Dee's first steady Pinellas County gig, at the Desert Ranch Inn on St. Petersburg Beach. He became a part-owner of the club.

of dance favorites and pop hits, and his oversized personality.

His first album, *Dee-Lightful!*, yielded a Top 20 hit in a Dee original called "Plantation Boogie." In his career, Dee would record 56 albums for Decca, and for the company that later absorbed it, MCA Records.

For more than a decade, he toured the country, picking up exclusive bookings in the nightclubs that could afford him. Even as rock 'n' roll swept America and the world, Dee's music – tuneful, toe-tapping, easy on the ears and unlikely to stir any kind of controversy – appealed enormously to one gently aging generation after another.

He appeared on all the TV shows – Ed Sullivan. Jack Paar. Arthur Godfrey. Mike Douglas. Lawrence Welk introduced him as "Denny Lee, the famous Chinese organ player," Dee used to say in his act.

Still, it was a grueling pace. "I got sick – exhaustion, nerves, hives," he recalled to an interviewer. "Went down to 120 pounds. The road tours got to me, one week here, two weeks there, carrying our equipment, eating in bed, traveling by truck." His first marriage crumbled in the midst of it.

In 1961, Dee met a Dutch beauty named Hendrica Koreman in a Ft. Lauderdale club. After they got married, they settled in Sarasota – he was a big draw at the prestigious Elbow Room club – and decided to make a more permanent home

1967 (l-r): Raymond, Georgia, Lenny and Henny. DeStoppelaire family collection.

near Tampa Bay.

(As a youngster, Leonard George DeStoppelaire spent summers visiting his grandparents in the Sulphur Springs neighborhood of Tampa, so he had a fondness for the area.)

Lenny and Henny (as they called each other) brought two children into the world – daughter Georgia and a son, Raymond – in the '60s, while Lenny was in semi-permanent residence at the Desert Ranch Inn on St. Petersburg Beach. He became part owner of the place and played there for six years.

Lenny Dee's Dolphin Den opened July 1, 1967, in the new Dolphin Village Shopping Center. He'd signed a 10-year lease with businessman W.W. Caruth, who was building the shopping center across Gulf Boulevard from his beach hotel, the Happy Dolphin Inn. "I'm going to make this into the west coast's most exciting supper club," Dee enthused to the *St. Petersburg Times*.

In advertisements for the 350-seat Den, he billed himself as *Nation's Top Organ Comic*. And no one was about to claim otherwise.

"St. Pete Beach was just a two-lane highway," recalls Georgia Dee. "There was the Don CeSar, and then it was just all beach until you got to the shopping center."

The show always began with a dance combo – sometimes two – before Lenny would take the stage, accompanied by a drummer (for many years it was Lenny Dee, Jr., his son from that first marriage) and a reel-to-reel tape recorder containing sound effects and background musicians. Dee triggered the tapes from his organ bench.

He also pioneered the use of tape delay – what is today known as looping – to create comic moments, and to make it sound as if there was more than just a single musician (or vocalist) on the stage.

During a good month – usually during the winter season – the club averaged about 5,000 paying guests. Dee was netting a half million dollars annually.

A brief history of the Hammond organ

Although Hammond organs had been around since the 1930s and '40s, first in churches – as a less-expensive substitute for the pipe organ – and then popularized by Ethel Smith and her "Tico" novelty pop records, the instrument became widely used in the '50s. Jazz keyboardist Jimmy Smith introduced blues notes, walking basslines and, in the context of a jazz combo, improvisation.

Smith's organ of choice was the versatile and dramatic Hammond B3, also used to great effect by Gregg Allman on the early Allman Brothers Band albums.

Booker T. Jones had been the first to play

Dee played organ during services at St John Vianney Catholic Church every Sunday. DeStoppelaire family collection.

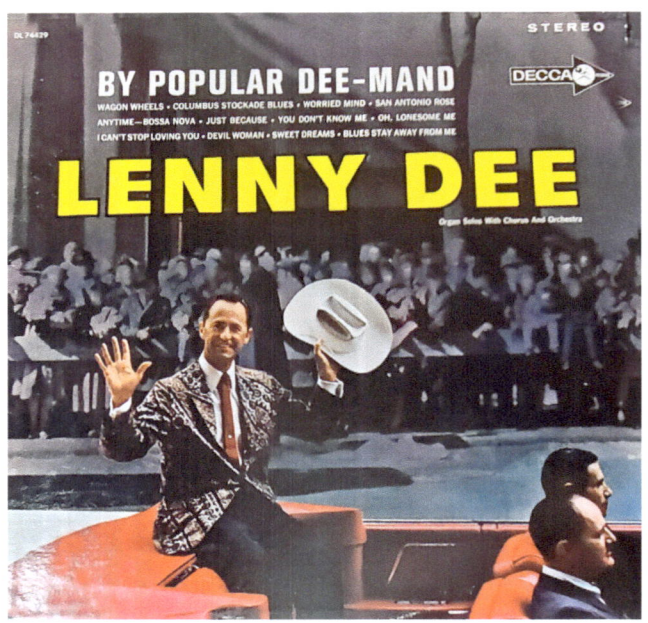

rock 'n' roll on a Hammond (think the 1962 smash "Green Onions"). Steve Winwood, Jon Lord (of Deep Purple), Keith Emerson (of the Nice and Emerson, Lake & Palmer) and Rick Wakeman were among the rock artists to make immensely creative use of the instrument.

According to the manufacturer, there was (and is) virtually no difference between the Hammond B3 and the C3, but the B3 became the "go-to" for jazz, rock and R&B. Lenny Dee played a half dozen different models, including the B3.

The Hammond's trademark vibrato effect was the result of a specialized revolving magnet and speaker – the Leslie – housed in a separate cabinet.

Reflecting on his early days in Nashville, "With an organ, man, there's no way," Dee said. "Organ was for a church or funeral home. I just kept playing that good rhythm. They kept me around because I could put people on the dance floor, playing whatever sounded good to me.

"I picked up a little comedy, a bit from this guy, and that guy. Just kept building."

The man and the music

There was nothing funny about his recordings – he played the music straight – unless you counted the eye-catching covers. The mid '50s albums, with punning titles like *Dee-Licious!*, *Dee-Latin* and *Mr. Dee Goes to Town*, featured Lenny hamming it up, pulling faces or dressed in wacky clothes. For his 1961 Christmas album (*Happy Holi-Dee*), he wore a Santa costume, the family's three miniature poodles on his lap.

The kicker has to be the jacket photo of 1962's *Down South*, the first album cut after he and Hendrica moved to St. Petersburg. Taken at Cypress Gardens, the tourist attraction near Winter Haven, it depicts Dee and his organ zipping along out on the lake, an outdoor motor attached to the back of his little platform. He's in full showman mode, dressed in a loud red blazer, his hands poised at the keyboard.

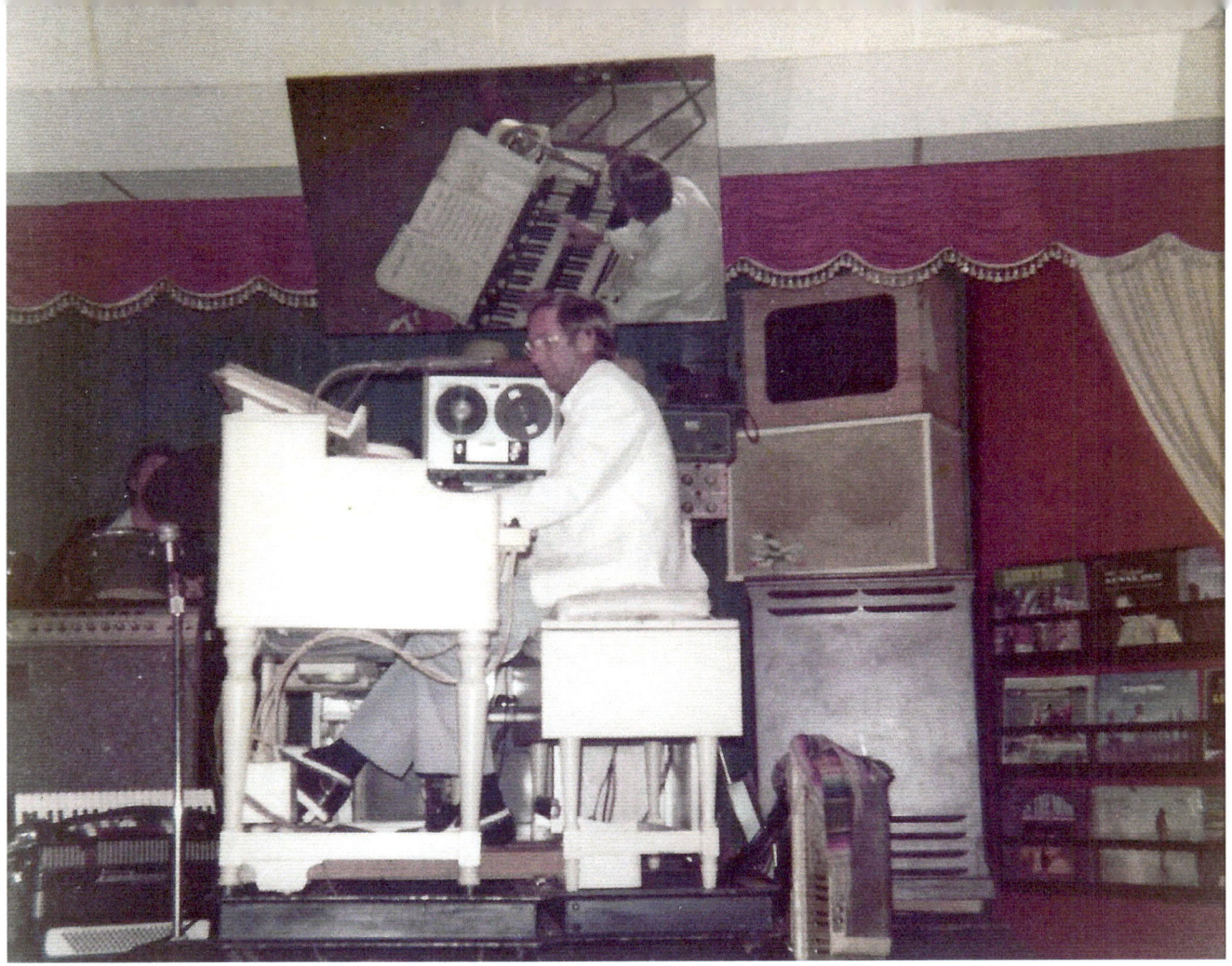

Onstage at his custom white Hammond Model A, Dolphin Den. Note the mirror, the accordion, the tape recorder and the rack of albums available for purchase. DeStoppelaire family collection.

And he's watching as a pretty girl on a waterski glides by, backwards. As if it were the most normal thing in the world.

Dee's records were strong enough sellers to keep him on the label for decades. He scored just one gold album – 1970's *Spinning Wheel* – but he religiously made the journey to Bradley's Barn recording studio in Nashville twice a year, each time to cut 11 new songs.

That translated into two albums a year. In the '60s, he covered mostly middle-of-the-road favorites like "Red Roses For a Blue Lady," "Born Free" and "I Left My Heart in San Francisco," while the next decade focused on the Top 40 pop charts and adult contemporary hits such as "I Write the Songs," "You Light Up My Life" and "What I Did For Love."

All of his albums were produced by country music legend Owen Bradley (Patsy Cline, Loretta Lynn, Conway Twitty). Guitarists Les Paul and Chet Akins appeared on his '50s records. By the late '60s, Bradley was adding lush strings and background singers for what was known as the "countrypolitan" sound.

Georgia says her father was a great procrastinator. "Maybe a week or two before the album was supposed to be cut, he would start saying 'I gotta play this song, I don't know this song.' He would listen to the record, of how they did the song, then he would just sit down and play it by ear. Then add his flair to it.

"He worked best under extreme pressure."

At home, Dee was a boat enthusiast (he proudly captained a 35-foot Hatteras Flying Dutchman with his name loudly painted on the side), and a licensed airplane pilot. There was, his daughter recalled, a dirt landing strip behind the Dolphin Village plaza. "We were always down at Albert Whitted," she says. "We would fly little Cessnas out of there. He had so many friends, and out on the beach we would go on a helicopter ride with one of his friends."

A devout Catholic, Dee played organ during services at St. John's every Sunday. He was fond of the occasional round of weekend golf.

"He was pretty introverted at home," explains Georgia Dee. "It depended on his moods. Sometimes we'd say 'oh, Dad's on a spending spree,' and he would go out and come home with all kinds of stuff. Big stuff, too – a new car, or a whole bunch of motorcycles for my brother. Or 'we're going on a trip,' and then off we'd go somewhere for a couple weeks."

Europe, South America, the Caribbean, every National Park in the U.S.A. – the Family DeStoppelaire took a lot of vacations. In California, they always got the VIP treatment at MCA-owned Universal Studios.

"We had chores at home – my brother would have to wash the boat, or wash the RV, cut the grass ... we were normal like that. At the restaurant, I was a cashier, a hostess, a salad girl, a busboy. We always had to work. My brother was in the kitchen as a chef. And we washed dishes. We did everything." Both kids graduated from St. Pete Catholic High School.

At the Dolphin Den, Dee appeared six nights a week, two 75-minute shows a night, for 11 months every year. "He was a very good man," says Georgia. "He had a real strong work ethic. And he never drank."

In 1978, after the 10 years were up, he left the supper club – and opened another one, the Kings Inn, on Treasure Island ("Home of the One-Pound Pork Chop").

Twenty years ago, places on the beach would be crowded till closing time. Today, midnight comes and you couldn't get them to watch Jesus Christ ride a bicycle on Gulf Boulevard. Tourists, you see, they want to get some rest so they can walk on the beach at 7 a.m.

Lenny Dee/St. Petersburg Times, March 6, 1984

Changing times

MCA Records' new boss pink-slipped every one of the label's easy listening artists in the late 1970s. Time, it seemed, had caught up with Lenny Dee. For the first time in 30 years, he was without a record contract.

Was his music hopelessly out of step? Strictly squaresville?

In 1984, the remodeled Kings Inn became Georgy's Supper Club, then Lenny Dee's

Supper Club. He announced his "semi-retirement," especially from the grueling nightly club schedule. When the Kings Inn lease ended, he dissolved his business, Lenny Dee's Dolphin Den, Inc. He moved to Tennessee and began making regular appearances on TV's Nashville Now.

Two years later, however, he was back in town, doing weekends at the Anchorage, the former Tierra Verde home to Guy Lombardo's long-ago Port-o-Call club.

"The New Lenny Dee Show" premiered at the Dolphin Beach Resort, three nights a week, in 1987. A move to the Coral Reef Resort happened in '91. Friday and Saturday nights.

He was officially an institution now, and still playing weeknight one-nighters in the likes of Spring Hill, or Sarasota, or New Port Richey. Sometimes he did demo shows for the Hammond company. "They used to call me the Suncoast's No. 1 son," he'd tell the audience. "Now they call me the old son of a beach."

In a 1997 interview with the Times, Dee bemoaned the lack of steady gigs and said he was selling a few of his beloved Hammond organs, dealing with arthritis and considering retirement. "I'm beginning to think God is telling me, Lenny, you've played long enough."

Still, he joked, "Better over the hill than under it."

He smiled at the reporter. "I never forget I've been there, had it all. I never forget I've been on top."

Nine years later, at age 83, he was gone.

"Down South" was the first album Lenny Dee recorded after relocating to Florida. This photo was taken at the Cypress Gardens waterski attraction in Winter Haven. Decca Records.

From Dartmouth, Nova Scotia, Hugh Boyd was 25 years old when he sailed for Tahiti aboard MGM film studio's replica HMS Bounty, in 1960. All photos in this chapter were discovered after Boyd's death in 2022.

Driving a rented Vespa scooter, Boyd periodically traveled to the other side of the island to secure cold beer for cast and crew, to be sold at a modest markup. His buddy (and future brother-in-law) Wayne Dewar likely took this photo.

Hugh Boyd and HMS Bounty in Tahiti

A man with an insatiable lust for adventure, Hugh Boyd spent much of his life as captain of *HMS Bounty*, the three-masted wooden sailing ship built for a Hollywood movie and moored in St. Petersburg, as a tourist attraction, for more than 20 years.

Every time *Bounty*, a working vessel that could travel under sail or via diesel engines, was called upon to travel somewhere on the globe, Hugh Boyd was ship's master.

He resigned when *Bounty*, after changing owners, left its permanent berth at the St. Pete Pier in the late 1980s (it would continue to return seasonally for another decade). And he began a second chapter as a mountain climber, scaling – so he told his family – every high peak in Colorado.

After his death on Jan. 26, 2022, at the age of 86, his children Tom Boyd and Tara Beesley began the emotional task of clearing out the St. Petersburg home Hugh shared with his beloved wife Sharon, who'd died in 2013.

It was in the attic – what her dad called the foc'sle (forecastle) – that Beesley discovered well-preserved boxes of photographs Hugh Boyd had taken over the years from various sojourns hither and yon.

There were more than 200 transparencies from the South Pacific Island of Tahiti, during the production of MGM's *Mutiny on the Bounty* in 1960 and '61, starring Marlon Brando, Trevor Howard and Richard Harris.

The studio had commissioned the ship's construction, in a Lunenberg, Nova Scotia shipyard, for what would be the third cinematic re-telling of an actual 1789 rebellion aboard a British military vessel in the South Seas.

Twenty-five-year-old Hugh Boyd, from the nearby town of Dartmouth, was one of 22 Nova Scotians who signed up for crew duty; also aboard was his buddy Wayne Dewar, 21, from Hantsport. Wayne's sister Sharon was Hugh's sweetheart. Under Captain Ellsworth Coggins, Hugh began as an able-bodied seaman, while Wayne was made mess boy, serving up food for the crew.

I signed on for Bounty mainly to get the adventure. It seems like a wonderful opportunity to get in the South Seas, which must be everyone's dream at one time or another. I can hardly wait to get there. They say those golden-skinned girls down there are really pretty.
Hugh Boyd to a CBC-TV interviewer/ September 1960

He wasn't far off – when *Bounty* sailed into Tahiti's Maatvai Bay on Dec. 3, after a 7,000-mile voyage plagued by stormy seas and a shipboard fire, the crew was greeted by hundreds of curious locals, many of them women, barefoot and beautiful and bearing flower leis to hang around the sailors' necks.

Bounty was a three-masted sailing ship, built from 18th century blueprints discovered in the British Admiralty archives. "I signed on for Bounty mainly to get the adventure," Boyd told National Geographic. "It seems like a wonderful opportunity to get in the South Seas, which must be everyone's dream at one time or another."

After three months at sea, this was quite a welcome sight for 22 young, healthy Canadian men.

But *Bounty* had arrived later than anticipated, after the Tahitian rainy season had started, so director Carol Reed (he would be replaced, later, by Lewis Milestone) shot what he could on dry days, with no ship in sight. MGM flew the film company back to England, for interior sequences. Actors, cameras etcetera would not return until March, after the rain stopped.

The company had laid down a rule about intimate fraternization with local females. But Brando, who famously did whatever

he pleased, studio be damned, held frequent parties at his rented villa during the entire shoot. Many days, he showed up on set late, hung over, and in a bad mood.

The crew, meanwhile, bunked aboard the anchored *Bounty*. And some of them got around.

Tom Boyd says he sometimes asked his old man about the experience. "In all the drunken conversations I had with him, when I asked if he'd fooled around in Tahiti, he'd say 'No … I don't remember.'"

Wayne Dewar, however, got close to a local girl named Teretiaiti Tevahineheipoua Maifano, who worked as a singer on a cruise ship based in the nearby city of Papeete. Everyone called her Suzanne. "Wayne met Suzanne on a moonlit patch of Tahitian beach," says Tom Boyd. "They fell in love, they say, at first sight."

But Uncle Wayne, remembers Tara Beesley, "was also a bugger. I remember at his funeral, there were three ex-wives. He loved wine, women and song, and none of them flat. Great uncle, terrible father. These guys were characters."

(Wayne and Suzanne married in Las Vegas, after Bounty had wrapped production, and settled in Nova Scotia. They divorced five years later.)

Once MGM returned, approximately 6,000 locals turned up to play "themselves" when filming commenced on the scene depicting *Bounty*'s arrival in Maatvai Bay. The Canadian crew members were tapped to play crewmen on the fictional *Bounty*, and other background roles.

"They asked the guys to grow out their hair and beards, so they could pass as rough and tumble characters," Tom Boyd reports. "And they actually dyed Dad's hair red so he could be in two different scenes. His hair was brown. They put a perm on him and dyed it red so he could pass for a different person altogether."

Because he looked particularly smart in a British naval uniform, Wayne was hired as Brando's stand-in.

They were 12-hour work days, six days per week. There was a lot of sitting around, sweltering in the Pacific Sun, while Brando sulked, or argued over script changes with the producer and director (this would be the most enduring legacy of *Mutiny on the Bounty*, which was released to lukewarm reviews in 1962).

On off hours, there wasn't much to do but explore, or nap, or throw the occasional shipboard party.

"Dad was full of energy," Tom Boyd explains, "so he hiked to the other side of the island, and in town he found a little place that sold beer, and a place that rented him a Vespa. So he started hauling beer back to the other side of the island.

"He convinced the cook to let him use the walk-in freezer, so he kept the beer cold and sold it for a tidy little profit. His beer was so popular that Marlon Brando specifically asked for Dad to bring him a cold one."

Twenty-two Bounty crew members were from Nova Scotia.

Hugh Boyd in the rigging.

(Years later, Tom says, Brando expressed a desire to purchase *Bounty* from the studio while it was in residence in St. Pete, and flew Hugh Boyd to California to talk about a transition. Nothing ever came of it.)

After sailing from Tahiti in mid-summer, *Bounty*, and the film company, stopped briefly in the Leeward Islands, Bora Bora and Hawaii for additional outdoor sequences. Although Hugh Boyd's photographs aren't dated, several seem to depict the area around Honolulu and other Hawaiian locales.

Curiously, few of the images show much in the way of cameras, or any of the other Ultra Panavision 70 widescreen equipment that had been hauled to the other side of the world. Similarly, few if any of the name actors appear amongst the photos.

Instead, Hugh – and his future brother-in-law, Wayne, who took the ones with Hugh in them – focused their early '60s lenses on their friends, and the day-to-day business of their life and work on the island. They depict casual moments on the beach, in the rigging, on the deck and belowdecks on Bounty, and include most of the crew in candid, free-spirited moments.

Both of Boyd's children believe these photos haven't been seen in decades. Their father certainly never mentioned them; he probably, they figured, forgot they even existed.

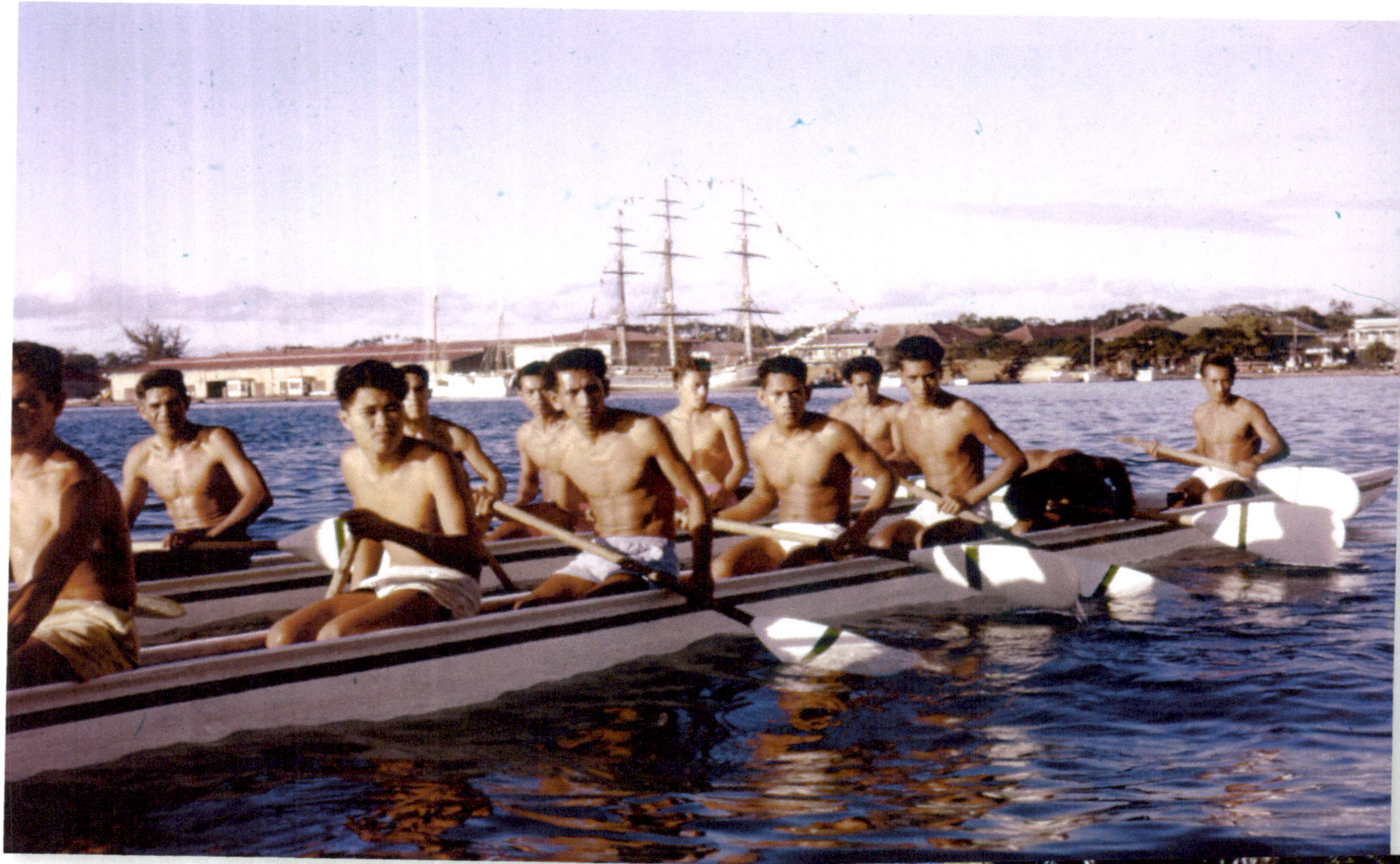

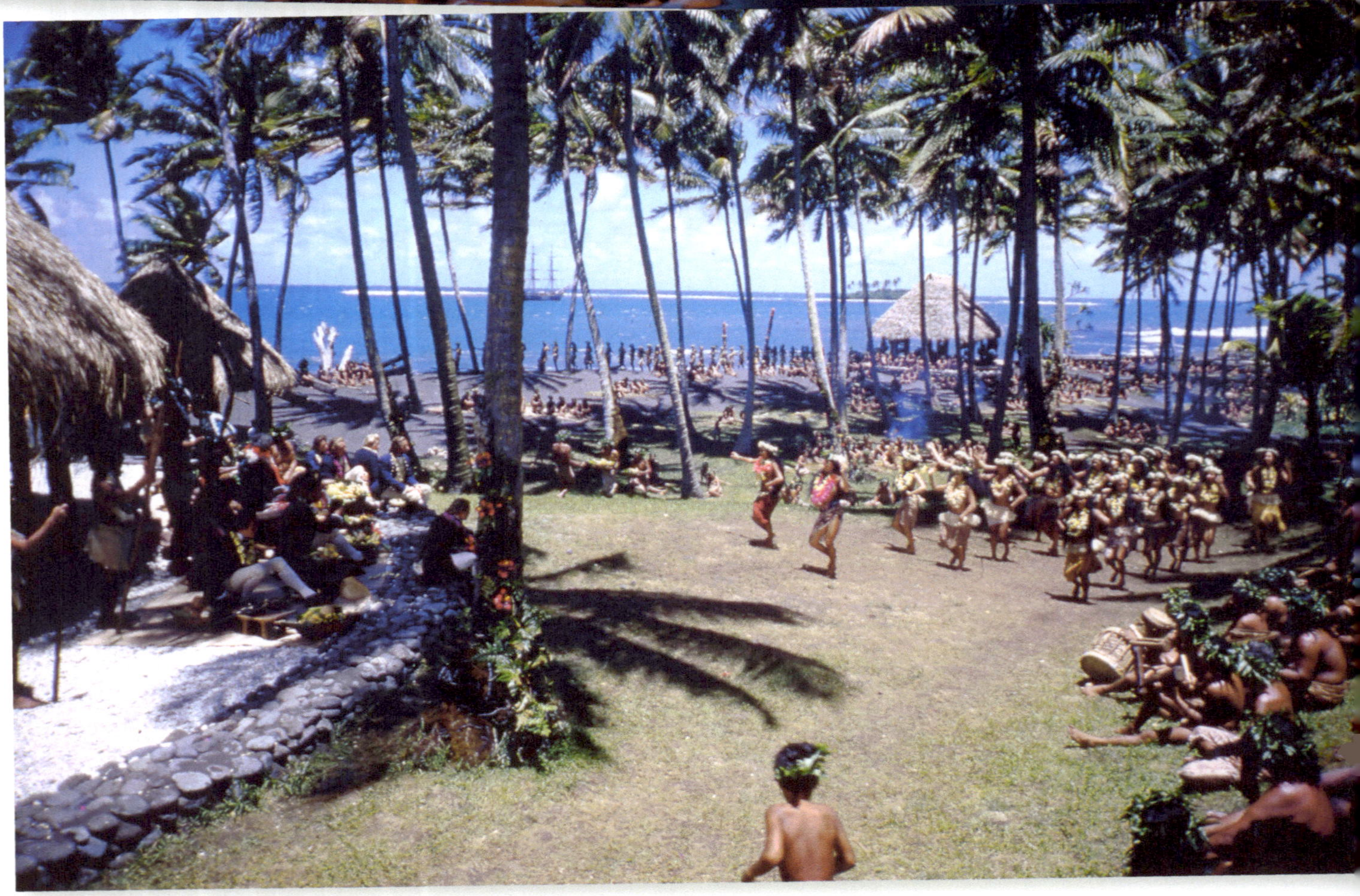

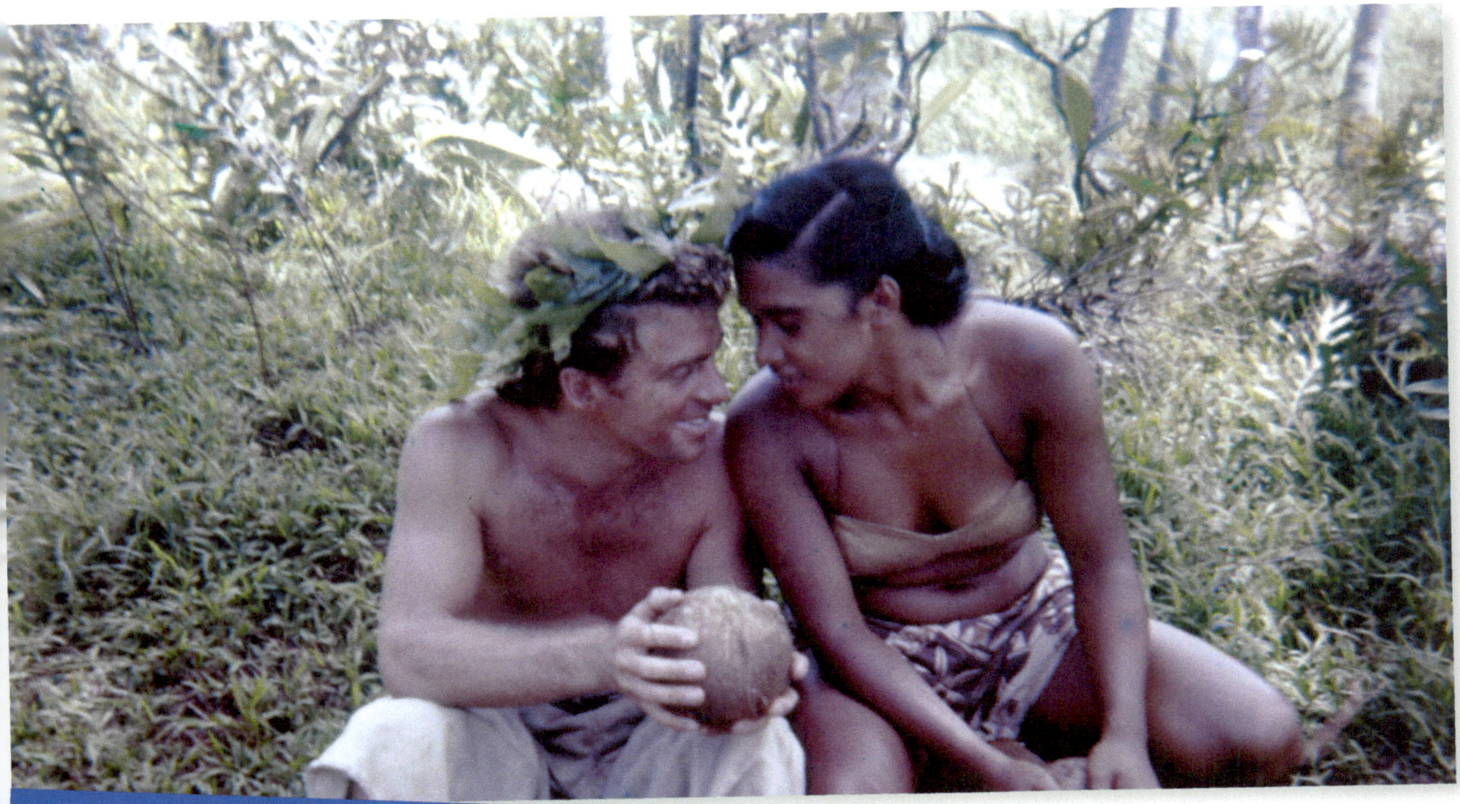

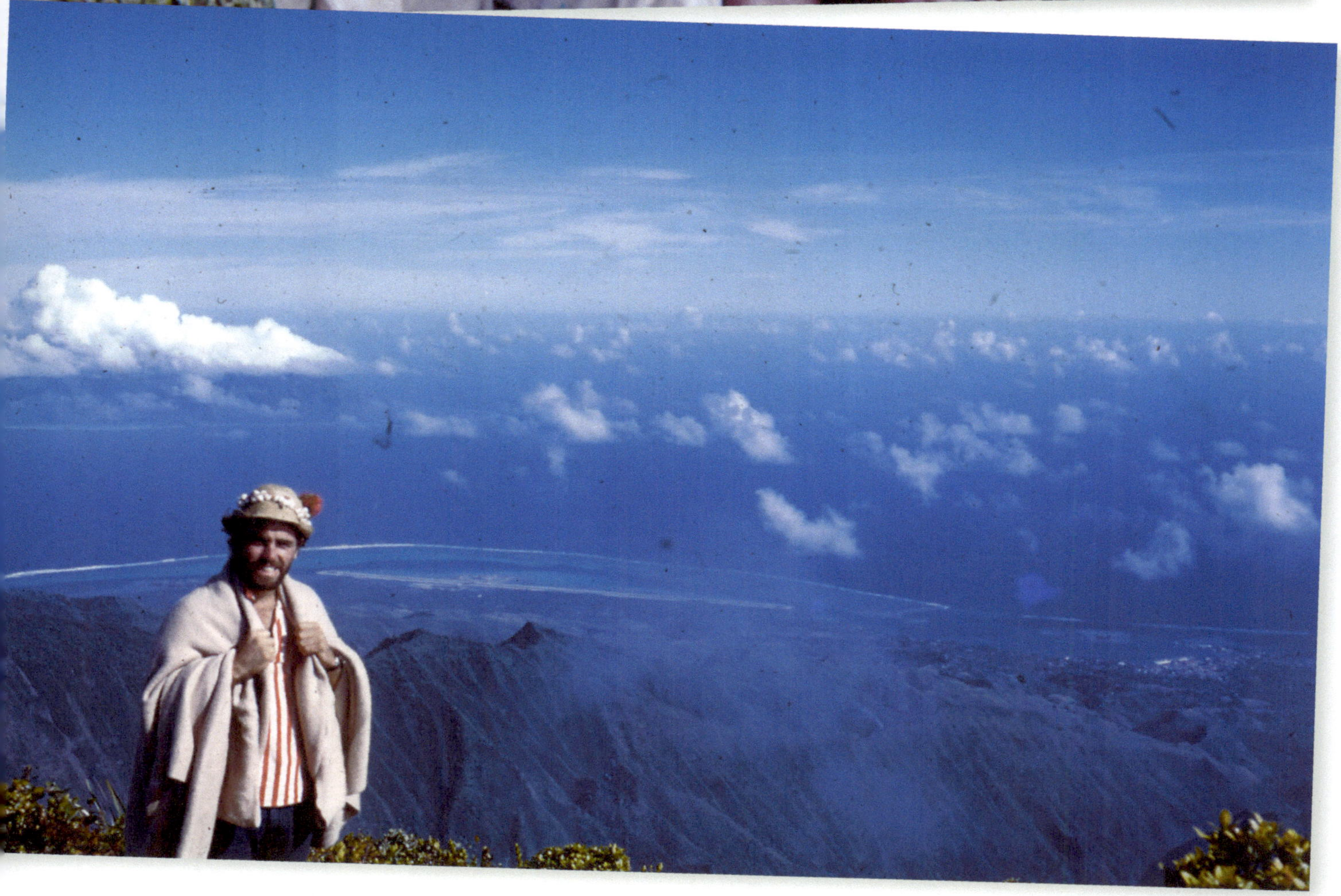

Cast, crew and Native extras fraternized often when they weren't needed on set.

Wayne Dewar, left, with Marlon Brando (center) and other cast members.

Florida Harvests the Nation's Humor

BUM STORIES

$3.95

Compiled by
O.A.T. — OF ALL THINGS
DICK BOTHWELL
St. Petersburg Times
Columnist

Cartoon by Dick Bothwell.

Times keeper: Columnist Dick Bothwell

hen it was announced that longtime *St. Petersburg Times* columnist Dick Bothwell had died, uncontrolled weeping reverberated throughout the storied, and normally stoic, newsroom. The public tributes poured in, including hundreds of letters, calls and in-person visits from readers, expressing shock and sorrow that a name and a face they'd known for four decades was, just like that, gone.

Although the newspaper wouldn't start to call itself the *Tampa Bay Times* for another 31 years, Bothwell's death on Jan. 30, 1981 was another in a series of signs that St. Petersburg's identity was changing. The innocence of the early decades was gone. The Sunshine Skyway Bridge had recently fallen – the area's first real tragedy. Webb's City, the gargantuan drugstore that had dominated downtown since the '30s, was closed and soon to be demolished. The crumbling Vinoy Park Hotel was populated with pigeons, rats and vagrants. And Nelson Poynter, the newspaper's owner and very public figurehead, a community booster, had died in 1978.

"For many of our readers, Dick Bothwell WAS the *St. Petersburg Times*," executive editor Robert Haiman said at the time.

Bothwell was a humorist whose folksy, Will Rogers-esque musings appeared in two regular columns, Of All Things (he called it OAT) and Brighten Up Mondays (a.k.a. BUM). Think Lewis Grizzard without the Southern cutesiness, or Dave Barry without the snark. Carl Hiaasen without the politics.

He wrote about Everyman, Everywoman and Everykid.

Cartoon by Dick Bothwell.

He was also a features writer, which meant he interviewed film and TV stars, lady wrestlers, comedians and circus acts, and reported on public events like park and pier dedications, the Festival of States, the Mutt Derby and the charity Fishathon. And a serious student of local history, which he wrote about with relish (and sometimes with mustard), always with tongue planted firmly in cheek.

Author and Poynter Institute writing coach Roy Peter Clark points out that the "dominant columnist" with a distinctive voice was a thing of great value in 20th century media. "Bothwell would never be that today," Clark says. "Or 20 years ago, even.

"But for the 1940s and '50s, and even into the '60s, he represented an era of life in St. Petersburg. Which, to the outside world, could be laughed at, as the city of the newly-wed and nearly-dead. As the world's largest open-air mausoleum."

However, Clark adds, "inside that world there were people coming here to retire, to leave the cold weather and crime-ridden cities behind … Dick was a Midwesterner, and St. Petersburg was a Midwestern town."

He knew his readers, and his readers got to know him.

Former *Times* writer Jeff Klinkenberg remembers Bothwell as "the last of his kind, a corny humorist and columnist who wrote every day, typing his stories with two fingers. He was of the front page era but without the alcohol, cigarettes, the swearing or dizzy blonds."

Like Clark, Klinkenberg joined the writing staff of "Florida's Best Newspaper" a few years before Bothwell's untimely exit at age 63. "He was loved by readers and his colleagues, whom he enjoyed teasing without mercy," Klinkenberg says.

In a lengthy, loving 1981 tribute, Bothwell's friend Bob Stiff, editor of the afternoon *Evening Independent* paper, had mused that perhaps Bothwell's old-school, molasses-slow humor made him something of an anachronism, particularly in a fast-paced contemporary newsroom.

"The young people didn't understand this man without a shred of sophistication, this man who wrote and told corny jokes, this man who never had a bad word to say about anyone, this man who always smiled and never seemed depressed," Stiff wrote. "They didn't understand his love for horehound drops, or his dislike for asparagus, either."

("That flabby green weed," Bothwell called it. "At last week's United Way dinner, the Bayfront Concourse had the bad taste to serve the stuff. There it ay, three limp, flaccid lengths of it, on a bed of lettuce. As an extreme courtesy, I ate it down, the United Way. Talk about giving").

Born in 1917, James Richard Bothwell grew up on his parents' homestead in tiny Alva, Wyoming – his father ran the general store – and then in nearby Lead, South Dakota, in the fabled Black Hills.

In 1939, with only a high school education, he answered an ad in *Time* magazine (a service many national publications provided after the Great Depression). Down in Florida, a place he'd only peripherally heard of, the *St. Petersburg Times* was looking for an editorial cartoorist.

As it happened, Bothwell's portfolio was impressive, and he was hired at $17.50 a week, for the *Times*' art department. For

They weren't all fascinating interviews, but Bothwell the reporter was always game: Here, he talks to banker CRF Wickenden about the Times' new pension plan for 1958. Tampa Bay Times/Zuma Press.

years, he constituted the entire department.

After a stint in the Army, he returned to St. Pete. That's when he began writing – first about the weather (sometimes as J. Thundersquall Drip) and, over time, about whatever struck his fancy.

St. Petersburg doesn't worry about growing older. It worries about growing younger, and even talks hysterically about buying itself a bikini, just to show folks.
Of All Things/ Nov. 23, 1962

Local lad has a sure-fire experience for "I've Got a Secret," if it's still on TV 20 years from now. "I fell off an elephant when I was 20 months old," he can tell the panel. Happened at Tampa's Lowry Park (Fairyland Divisions) Sunday afternoon. The idea is, kids pose atop this young elephant, by climbing up a ladder on one side. A chimp poses too, sitting on the elephant's head.
Of All Things/Jan. 26, 1967

Without fail, his columns ended with some groan-inducing joke. Bothwell regularly received jokes in the mail from readers, and proudly stole from the best (and almost always gave credit where it was due).

How did the pig get to the top of the Empire State Building? Simple. The swine flew.

It was so cold when I was born, I was delivered by a penguin instead of a stork.

Know what you get when you cross a black widow spider and a horse? I don't either, but if it bites you, you can always ride it to the hospital.

Bothwell and his wife June bought their first St. Pete home on the south side, adjacent to Lake Maggiore. In the days before the county employed professional trappers to capture and kill nuisance alligators, average citizens caught the reptiles, drove to the 327-acre site and released them (and no, it didn't always work out so well).

Bothwell, as was his nature, was curious about the animals that proliferated in his back yard. So he researched, and he learned, and he wrote columns about alligators. In 1962, through the *Times*-owned Great Outdoors Publishing Co., he wrote and illustrated *The Great Outdoors Book of Alligators and Other Crocodilia*.

Bespectacled, tall and gawky even into his 60s, the toupee-sporting columnist liked to say he was often mistaken for actor Robert Redford, and for emphasis would replace his own OAT photo with that of the handsome Hollywood star.

Just like Orson Wells, I will tell no joke before its time, and a good many after. But in truth, there is no such thing as a bad joke. This rumor was started ages ago by people who could not think of their own jokes.

Of All Things/Nov. 12, 1979

On the occasion of his 40th anniversary with the paper, Bothwell – the office jokester - was uncharacteristically serious: "I've written about all sorts of characters," he wrote, "but the person I like to write about the most is an older person who has done something with their later years. I feel this is a terrific inspiration to all the older people who think that their useful days are gone."

To illustrate a column he'd written about cowboys, cattle and life in frontier towns, Bothwell wore a full complement of western regalia to work the afternoon of Thursday, July 29, 1981. After a studio session with staff photographer Tony Lopez, he entertained his fellow journalists with a few clumsily-executed rope tricks and a hatful of bad jokes.

Friday morning, he woke up with chest pains. A devout Christian Scientist, Bothwell refused to consult a doctor. He sat down in his favorite living room chair, suffered a massive heart attack, and was gone.

Jan. 29, 1981: To illustrate a new story, Bothwell wore a cowboy outfit to work. He died at home the next morning (the column was published posthumously). Tampa Bay Times photo by Tony Lopez/ZUMA Press.

Sports editor Hubert Mizell wrote an epitaph for Bothwell: "Newspapers are, by necessity, tough places. Every day, there are stories of pain, bleeding, calamity and death. People have jobs doing nothing but writing about people who have died. But on Friday there was an air around our shop that I had not sensed in 23 years in the business.

"Difficult, but a tribute to the man."

Oct. 29, 2019: Jonathan Styles (son of Officer Jerry Styles), Officer Leon Jackson, Tatiana Killen (daughter of Officer Primus Killen) and Chief Anthony Holloway dedicate the plaque honoring the Courageous Twelve at SPPD headquarters. St. Petersburg Police Department.

Fight for right: The Courageous Twelve

hat the St. Petersburg Police Department did was to superimpose on natural geographic zones an artificial zone that rests on the Department's judgment of Negroes as a class. The Department concluded that Negroes as a class are suitable only for the zone appropriately numbered 13. This is the kind of badge of slavery the thirteenth amendment condemns.

U.S. Court of Appeals for the Fifth Circuit/August 1, 1968

And thus BAKER et al., Plaintiffs, v. CITY OF ST. PETERSBURG came to an end, in favor of the plaintiffs – all 12 Black uniformed officers of the St. Petersburg Police Department.

They sued in 1965, the year after President Lyndon B. Johnson signed the Civil Rights Act into law, because they believed the city was still operating under the unspoken Jim Crow guidelines of an earlier era, when equality, sadly, meant different things to different members of society.

Black officers were only allowed to patrol the area known as Zone 13 – encompassing the Deuces (22nd Street South), the Gas Plant, Methodist Town and what was left of Pepper Town, the city's first Black settlement.

Black neighborhoods.

Neither could Black officers arrest white suspects, wherever they might be apprehended. They could detain them, put in a call and wait for a white officer (there were 250 of them) to make the collar.

The reason, (white) Chief of Police Harold Smith said, was simply that Black officers could "do a better job" in Black neighborhoods.

No, it's racial discrimination, pure and simple, cried the officers, adding that they were routinely given raggedy old cruisers to drive, while the Caucasian cops always seemed to get the new cars. And their lockers were all located in a row together, implying, they claimed, that were "equal, but separate."

Today, we know them as the Courageous Twelve, and their story represented a major breakthrough in race relations not only on a local level, but across the entire country. They were the first to speak out. And the first to act.

Concluded the U.S. Court of Appeals: *Nothing we say is intended to suggest that the Negro officers on the police force of St. Petersburg should be given preferential treatment. They deserve only what they seek — equality.*

Says St. Petersburg Police Chief Anthony Holloway: "They really changed the face of law enforcement. They put their careers on the line so that people like me were able to move up in the law enforcement community. That meant a lot to all of us – not just St. Pete, but nationwide."

Leon Jackson, 82, is the last surviving member of the Courageous Twelve. He was the youngest of the group, most of whom grew up in St. Petersburg, graduated from Gibbs High School and were proud to be civil servants.

Of course, suing their employer was a risky move. "We knew what we were getting into," Jackson says. "We knew we could have been fired. But somebody had to take the chance to change the system."

It would have been easier to keep their mouths shut, just as police officers in other cities were surely doing. "All of us were scared. We could have lost our homes. We could have lost our jobs. Our bills wouldn't get paid. We'd be out looking for work. And they could have blackballed us out of law enforcement."

They began to meet, just the 12 of them, in one another's homes. "And out of one of those meetings," Jackson recalls, "we said 'Look, let's request a meeting with the chief, and discuss it with him.' So the chief met with us twice – and of course he didn't do anything about our complaints. We requested a third meeting, and he refused to meet with us any more."

RACIAL DISCRIMINATION CHARGED

12 Negro Patrolmen Sue St. Petersburg

ST. PETERSBURG — Twelve St. Petersburg Negro patrolmen yesterday filed suit in Federal District Court in Tampa charging the St. Petersburg Police Department with racially discriminatory practices. It specifically cites discrimination in the areas of work assignments, promotion and pay, disciplinary procedures and use of dressing room facilities.

Named defendants in the suit are the City of St. Petersburg, City Manager Lynn Andrews as administrative head of city departments and agencies, and Police Chief Harold Smith.

Although only 12 of 16 Negro employes of the police department are listed as plaintiffs, the suit is a class suit, filed "on behalf of others similarly situated" — that, is, all Negro employes of the St. Petsbirg Police Department.

ly $8-million outstanding on the federally insured mortgage.

'Work-Study' Slated

The Gibbs campus of St. Petersburg Junior College plans to establish a federally financed "work-study" program in September to partially replace the discontinued National Defense Student Loan Fund (NDSL).

Pinellas County School Supt. Floyd Christian has called a press conference for 9:30 a.m.

In the 1960s, Leon Jackson was the youngest member of the Courageous Twelve. At 82, he is the last survivor. St. Pete Catalyst.

Was that to be the end of it?

"Our theory was that he wasn't going to change. When he met with us, the only thing he would say was 'I'll get back with you guys.' But he didn't give any concrete reason for it, or say if he was going to make any changes."

The frustrated officers then consulted attorney James B. Sanderlin, who'd been working civil rights cases locally for several years. Jackson: "Freddie Crawford was our leader, and he said 'Let's sue 'em.' We told Freddie 'Look, man, you're putting us on the spot. We could get suspended, or even fired.' And Freddie was, I don't want to say militant, but he was very steadfast. And he said 'I don't care. Let's file a lawsuit. The chief's not going to do anything.'"

A potential silver lining was discussed. "One of the officers – I don't recall who – said 'You know, the colored people are not going to stand for them firing us ... but if they fire us, so be it.'"

Someone asked if maybe they should think it over before voting. "And Officer Charles Holland said "There's nothing to think about.' So we voted, right then and there. And all 12 of us agreed."

Sanderlin filed the suit May 12, 1965 in Federal District Court in Tampa. Defendants named were Police Chief Smith and City Manager Lynn Andrews. It cited discrimination in the areas of work assignments, promotion and pay, disciplinary procedures and use of dressing room facilities.

"We could not work any desk job inside the station," Jackson recalls. "We could not even take the sergeants' exam for a promotion."

Police sergeant Sam Jones, who was Black, "could only supervise the African-American officers," Jackson says. "He could not supervise the white officers."

Jones and two detectives were the only other Black police department employees. All three declined to join the uniformed officers in their litigation.

The 12 had no issues with white officers, explains Jackson. For the most part, at least on the record, everyone got along great.

But the Black officers didn't discuss the lawsuit with their white counterparts. "To them, it would be a sensitive subject. Some of them wouldn't accept it. And some of them, not all, felt that we were against them – but we were not. We were against the system.

"One Caucasian police officer, his name was Bob Stokes, he went to federal court and testified that we were treated separately from the white officers. He supported us."

In March, 1966, a federal district judge sided with the city and dismissed the case; Sanderlin, with the added support of the NAACP, both publicly and financially, appealed.

Not long before the appeals court overturned the lower verdict, Chief Smith began to quietly make changes. To show the community, Jackson believes, that the department was listening.

Jackson was the first officer assigned to patrol a traditionally white neighborhood – Snell Isle and Shore Acres. On the midnight-to-dawn shift.

"My theory is that they chose those neighborhoods because that's where the more educated whites lived," says Jackson, "and the wealthy whites. And they felt they would accept me more. And I didn't have any problems."

Once the appeal passed, change came slowly – but indeed it came. "After the appeal, they had to do it. Officer Raymond DeLoach went to work on the front desk. And I think the city attorney probably told them to do that, to show people there was a change."

Jackson left the force in 1972 and went on to a lengthy career in windshield-film technology. Several others followed similar career trajectories.

Officer Horace Nero was promoted to sergeant, and officers Raymond DeLoach, Johnnie B. Lewis, Primus Killen and Charles Holland made detective.

James Sanderlin became Pinellas County's first African-American judge.

In 2007, *St. Petersburg Times* reporter Jon Wilson wrote a story, "Pioneering policemen," and Jackson, who had all but for-

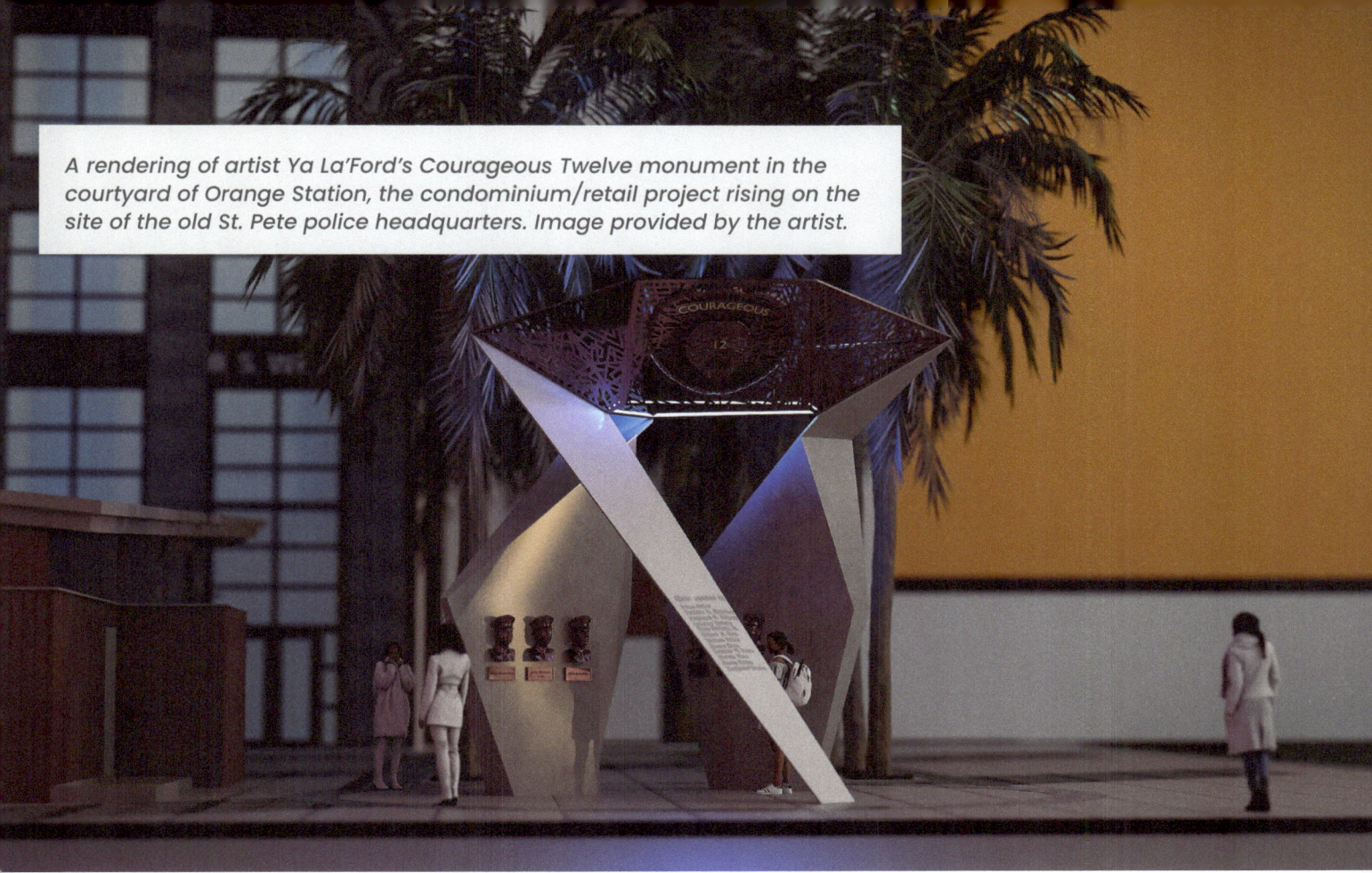

A rendering of artist Ya La'Ford's Courageous Twelve monument in the courtyard of Orange Station, the condominium/retail project rising on the site of the old St. Pete police headquarters. Image provided by the artist.

gotten about the case, took it upon himself to bring all the survivors together.

"Once it hit the news media, it went like wildfire," he remembers. The Courageous Twelve were profiled in newspapers and on TV news shows the world over – even Al Jazeera wrote about them. They were honored at an NAACP banquet, given the keys to the City of St. Petersburg and celebrated at the Carter G. Woodson Museum.

As the last survivor, Jackson was Grand Marshall of the city's Martin Luther King Jr. parade, and was present when a plaque honoring the Courageous Twelve was unveiled by Chief Holloway at the new St. Pete Police Headquarters. He subsequently authored a book, *Urban Buffalo Soldiers: The Story of St. Petersburg's Courageous Twelve.*

Noted sculptor and painter Ya La'Ford was commissioned to create a memorial to the dozen who dared in the courtyard of Orange Station, the $80 million condominium/retail project under construction on the site of the old St. Pete police headquarters at 1302 Central Ave.

The 20-foot sculpture, made of bronze, concrete and stainless steel, will include La'Ford's signature geometric patterns, along with relief busts of all 20 officers. It's to be an open, walk-through monument with a roof designed to look like a policeman's cap, complete with badge.

THE COURAGEOUS TWELVE: Adam Baker; Freddie L. Crawford; Raymond L. DeLoach; Charles Holland; Leon Jackson; Robert V. Keys; Primus Killen; James King; Johnnie B. Lewis; Horace Nero; Jerry Styles; Nathaniel L. Wooten.

Lead guitarist Ronnie Garvin was Stranger's hard-rocking secret weapon. Bridget Burke.

From the back jacket of Stranger's 1982 Epic Records album. From left: Tom "King" Cardenas, John Price, Greg Billings and Ronnie Garvin.

Stranger things: A rock 'n' roll saga

or a moment in time – one brief, shining, freeze-frame of a moment – it looked like Stranger was going to be the next Florida rock band to break big.

It was 1982, and Epic Records, riding high on platinum success with Jacksonville's Molly Hatchet, was throwing its considerable muscle behind Stranger's first album. It was produced in Los Angeles by the same guy who'd crafted million-sellers for Cheap Trick, Ted Nugent, REO Speedwagon – and Molly Hatchet. The world was Stranger's oyster.

Greg Billings, the lead singer and tireless, charismatic frontman for Stranger, thinks about that moment a lot these days. In his mid 60s, Billings is slim, trim and in good health, and still singing with as much power as he did in his 20s (the long curly hair, however, is gone forever).

The Stranger saga is fraught with "what might have beens" like the Epic Records launch.

The record (*Stranger*) came out and ... nothing. Didn't sell, didn't produce a hit single, didn't get Billings and his bandmates on MTV. The world yawned and looked away.

In retrospect, Billings believes famed producer Tom Werman rushed them – a bunch of Deep South rubes who knew

Billings at center stage. Epic Records.

zilch about making records – in and out of Epic's L.A. studio. At that point, they would have agreed to anything, just to get noticed. "This thing was fast, it was thin, it was just f—king awful," Billings says.

"I thought 'I don't think we sound like that,' but we were proud of what we did. We went out on tour, and we were great live, but the feedback was that the record was not a very good representation of the band." Epic dropped them; it took a while for the band to untangle itself from the red tape of bad management.

But they survived, and they flourished. Based out of Tampa Bay, Stranger had a good 15-year run as one of the top club acts in Florida and Georgia before calling it quits in 1996.

They self-produced a couple of albums, selling them on vinyl and cassette out of their tour bus after shows. "But," Billings says, "we could never capture what Stranger did live."

What they did was taut, powerful rock 'n' roll, riff-laden and full of hooks, the kind of tough stuff Sammy Hagar sang with Montrose, and David Lee Roth with Van Halen. Or Bon Scott with AC/DC. Heavy rock that wasn't heavy metal. Crunchy, good-time singalongs like "Jackie's So Bad," "Swamp Woman" and "Get On Up." They were also selling a lifestyle and an attitude.

Stranger's secret weapon was blonde guitarist Ronnie Garvin, a "chick magnet" (to use the parlance of the times) and a real shredder; Ronnie's strutting stage presence and incendiary solos were as key to the band's draw as Billings' vocals and gymnastics.

The band's origins were Texan – bassist Tom "King" Cardenas, from Austin, was the anchor for a hard rock outfit called KOKO (it's a boxing reference) that relocated in the late 1970s to the Atlanta area. The appetite for heavy bands, in rock clubs, biker joints and beach bars, was insatiable, and by the time KOKO had become a Florida favorite, playing up and down the peninsula, the name had been changed to Lynxx. John Price played drums.

In Charleston, S.C., local hotdog guitarist Ronnie Garvin talked his way into an onstage jam with Lynxx. "We did 'Tie Your Mother Down' by Queen," remembers Cardenas, "and he just nailed it. He must have been 19 – 'wow, this kid's good.'" Later, when the band's guitar player went back home to Texas, Cardenas and Price called Garvin, who right away hopped on a Greyhound bus to join the band during an in-progress week of gigs in Alabama.

The band changed its name again, to Romeo.

Greg Billings was 22 years old in 1979, down from his North Carolina hometown with an outfit called Merlin, playing Foghat, Rush and UFO covers in a Madeira Beach bar. "The band split up when we were in Florida, and so I came here and never left," he remembers.

At Skip's House of Rock and Roll, he was impressed with Romeo. "I'd watched them all week, and they did a 20-minute Montrose medley. All stuff from the first Montrose record, and I had that 8-track. I'd stand in front of the mirror and pose and sing those Sammy Hagar tunes. So I had 'em all down."

When Cardenas, Garvin and Price asked Billings to fill in while their singer took a break, he said yes – if I can do the Montrose medley. "I'd watched them do it three times, so I knew it." And he killed it. Everyone felt the chemistry in the room.

They asked Billings to join then, but he declined, explaining that he had another band project in the works. He was living in Madeira with his girlfriend and taking things slow.

"The beach life was too crazy for me," Billings laughs. "The Quaaludes days, and 151 rum. We'd get paid on Friday and stay drunk till Monday. We'd either go back to the job on Monday or quit the job, take that week off and then look for a job later in the week. Because back then, you'd just look in the paper for a job. Show up, the guy would hire you, and you'd work a week."

Over time, however, his new band failed to materialize, the money ran out, and Billings and his girlfriend returned, broke, to Winston-Salem. "And the day she dumped me, I went home and was getting ready to go sob in my bedroom. My mom goes 'Some guy named Tom King from Romeo called, and wants you to call him.' I'd given him my number on a napkin, and he'd kept it."

Within a few days, he was back in Florida and singing with Romeo. "I got there on Monday, and we played that night," Billings marvels "And we were together 15 years after that."

As Cardenas remembers it, six months had passed since that magical Montrose afternoon. Romeo's singer exited stage left, and the three remaining band members – him, Price and Garvin – were living in a cheap Tampa motel during yet another weeklong club residency. During the afternoons, they auditioned new singers. The only phone was in the motel office.

"I called up to Winston-Salem, where Greg was at. His brother answered and said Greg was out playing golf. When he called me back I asked him if he wanted to come down and play with us. He said 'Hell yeah.'

"I said all right, we'll send you a plane ticket. We got a gig in a week at the Level 3 Lounge in Orlando."

Romeo at that time had very few originals – and at Billings' insistence, they began to write. "And we wrote some shit songs," Billings laughs. "They were really bad. But a lot of people remember them, even the shitty ones. But we wrote a couple good ones, and we drew enough women to get a record deal." The name was changed to Stranger before the ill-fated Epic album was finished.

Cardenas likes the record. "For me personally, it was great. I was proud of everything we did. Actually, I thought we'd probably go a lot further."

The bassist blames the album's failure on promotion (none) and personal management (poor). Stranger was – in those early years – handled by Georgia-based rock manager Pat Armstrong, who had a handful of heavy-hitter clients.

"He had Molly Hatchet and he had Quiet Riot," Cardenas explains. "And he took care of Quiet Riot before he took care of us, you know?"

After that major label disappointment, the four band members returned to Florida, and soon became the darlings of the rock 'n' roll club circuit. In those days, you'd land in a city – Winter Haven or Daytona or Bradenton or St. Augustine – and play for five nights at the ABC Lounge, or Crown Liquors, at Jerry's Rockin' Disco, Fern Park Station or the 701 South. There was always another club in another town.

In 1984, in Gainesville, Tom Petty – home visiting friends and family, with Heartbreakers drummer Stan Lynch in tow – jumped onstage at a new club called The Islands and played a couple of songs with Stranger. It was the only time in his life the rock legend ever did anything like that.

To say that Stranger amassed a large and loyal following – particularly among women – is like suggesting the Beatles wrote a couple of catchy tunes. Stranger worked hard to become the biggest fish in a not-so-little pond.

They never got rich, and they never got traditionally "famous." But they were doing what they loved. "When we traveled a lot together, we had fun together, but we were f—kin' wild," Billings recalls. "I can't believe we lived through all that. Good thing we had a drummer that didn't drink; he drove after gigs. Tom always drove to the gigs. There's no way I'm driving."

They added a fifth member, keyboard

player Randy Holt, who lasted for a few years. By 1996, Stranger was back to the original foursome, playing the club circuit over and over again. They made more albums, self-produced and self-distributed.

But music, and the music business, was changing. It was the arrival of the Seattle grunge scene, Billings says, that caused him to begin thinking that Stranger – or at least their 1980s business model – was an anachronism.

Cardenas: "We did everything equally. Like songwriting – everybody's name was under all the songs. That way, we would all stay happy and stay together. Because a lot of bands will start arguing about royalties, and that'll get band members at each other. Our bus, our tractor trailer, the road crew, everything we paid for came off the top. And what was left, we split evenly."

Still, "I saw the writing on the wall for the last couple of years we were together," Billings says. "The crowds were getting smaller. We weren't getting along. If it was a week between gigs, we wouldn't talk and we wouldn't rehearse.

"I tried to tell them. I said we need to change, guys, we're doing things wrong. Bands didn't have trucks any more. Bands didn't have their own p.a. Bands didn't have four guys in the road crew any more. You carried your own gear, you showed up for gigs, you set it up and you played."

It all came to a head on Feb. 1, 1996. "I said 'Look around! Things aren't going good!' But they didn't want to hear it. I started screaming and yelling one night, and they said 'If you don't like it, f–kin' quit.' It was one of those things. I said 'OK, I will.' It was a dick move on my part.

"And right in the middle of our last show – I was drinking, I was fired up – I said 'I changed my mind, if you guys want we'll try to work this out.' Not knowing they'd already hired somebody else."

Replaced in his own band. "I'll be honest, it hurt a little bit," Billings says. "I drove home thinking about it, and my wife said 'It's probably for the best. Let's move on, Greg.'"

And move on he did. He was tending bar at a club on US 19 called Gasoline Alley while the "new" Stranger was onstage. "I didn't care. I just wanted to make some money."

Without Billings, however, Stranger lost its audience. The band finished for good three months after he left.

By then, Billings had joined another outfit, Damn the Torpedoes, which would eventually morph into the Greg Billings Band.

But there were darker times ahead.

Ronnie Garvin had been showing signs of serious depression, Billings remembers, during the last years of Stranger. He'd said some bizarre and disconcerting things. "I think he thought drinking made him numb. We all drank at night, but we didn't drink during the day. As soon as we started playing, we started having drinks. But man, you start drinking during the day, by nighttime you can't play.

"In the early days, Ronnie could drink and

play all night, but when he started drinking during the day and tried to play all night, it was not good."

The rumor was that Garvin's ex-wife was threatening to leave Florida, and take their two children. And then, Stranger – a 15-year commitment – was simply gone.

"I was in Damn the Torpedoes when he came to a gig," Billings says. "I told him, I said 'Ronnie, we could have been doing this together.' The place was packed. A beach crowd, little small joint, just packed. We were playing covers, we were playing Stranger tunes, we were having a blast.

"I think he was with Tom. They'd been fishing that night and they stopped in. And Ronnie didn't look good. He mentioned that he was going to go to Nashville or something. I didn't mean to make him feel bad, I just said 'If we'd only known what we were doing, we could be doing this together. You could have been in this band.' But obviously, he couldn't be in it now. I said 'I've got brothers I'm playing with now.' And that's the last time I saw him."

A week later – on Oct. 7, 1996 – Garvin took his life with a 10-gauge shotgun, at his Safety Harbor apartment.

"I knew it was coming," Billings says softly. "When I got the call, I was not surprised. I was sad. I was hurt. But I wasn't surprised."

Drummer John Price died of cancer in 2013.

Billings' bands, which almost always include Tom "King" Cardenas on bass, play plenty of Stranger's songs, for those who want to remember. For those who want to stand in the dark and experience that glorious, dizzy, uninhibited rock 'n' roll thing one more time.

In their element, onstage somewhere in Florida. Christopher Lee Helton.

They have more friends, many of them from the old days, than they can count.

Scars, sure. Regrets? Not a one.

"It was a great ride, as people say these days," says Cardenas. "I really enjoyed it. We all had a lot of fun."

Billings is circumspect. "It would be stupid for me to say I wouldn't do anything different," he says. "Because I think if we'd taken ourselves a little more seriously ... but then, that's why people liked us. If we'd done that, we might not have been as popular as we were."

"It would be stupid for me to say I wouldn't do anything different," Billings says today. "Because I think if we'd taken ourselves a little more seriously ... but then, that's why people liked us. If we'd done that, we might not have been as popular as we were." Bridget Burke.

The Headlights with Byrds legend Roger McGuinn in 1991, before their cross-county concert tour. Faune Walker.

From left: Steve Connelly, Steve Robinson, Danny DiPietra and Scott Dempster. Faune Walker collection.

When we were kings: The Headlights

or all of the 1980s and the first half of the '90s, the bay area band to beat was The Headlights. The group's closest competition, in terms of large, fanatical fan base and bronze badge of "almost famous" glory, was the hard-rocking, tough-talking Stranger.

The Headlights played '60s-style rock and power-pop – short, punchy, melodic songs, many of them self-penned ... and for the bulk of their run had no close competitors in that category.

When the first flush of melody-minded "new wave" music arrived in the late '70s, skinny ties and all, the Headlights turned on: Elvis Costello, Nick Lowe & Rockpile, Squeeze, the Cars, Talking Heads. All economy, no excess. Don't bore us, get to the chorus.

They continued to evolve, and as they did huge crowds came to Clancy's, Club Detroit and the ACL Club in St. Pete. The Masquerade in Ybor. Dance clubs in Clearwater, Dunedin, Tarpon, Lakeland, Orlando. The Headlights once played a solid month in Gainesville, with its notoriously picky music fans.

From the early, figuring-it-out days to the final flush of glory on top of the local music hierarchy, the band's main songwriter was guitarist and co-lead singer Steve Connelly.

"We were the first band to actually go out playing originals and getting booked," he recalls. "Nobody thought you could do it. I refused to do what was popular, Top 40 covers. We stuck to our guns and we started building this thing up. And from that, all the other bands, the whole scene here, opened up."

Perhaps the Headlights' biggest claim to fame – and what Connelly, in retrospect, realizes was their high-water mark – was playing behind former Byrd Roger McGuinn (then a bay area resident) on a cross-country tour during 1991. With McGuinn, they even opened for megastars ZZ Top in Stockholm, Sweden.

THE HEADLIGHTS

The Headlights begat Deloris Telescope, Mad For Electra, Multicolor House and other popular "quirky" pop-rock bands of the era and beyond. The ripples spread and are still felt today. "We spawned that whole scene," Connelly pronounces proudly. "That all started from the Headlights, doing originals."

"We never would have had any of it happen if it wasn't for Scott Dempster," observes Connelly. "Scott was a rock 'n' roll star; that's all he ever wanted to be. He would try to get backstage at any big shows."

Dempster, the Headlights' ever-enthusiastic bassman, ran into McGuinn behind the scenes at a Bob Dylan concert in 1988, and began chatting him up.

"Scott says 'Hey man, we're going into this studio next week. Why don't you come produce us?'

"And Roger goes 'Yeah, OK.'"

Simple as that. "We worked at the old Hitmakers in Tampa, which is now Morrisound Studios. And Roger drove his Volkswagen camper van there every day, from Indian Rocks Beach, to hang out with us and produce the four-song EP that we did, *Earthbound*. He really didn't do much – he hung out with us and made suggestions." Nevertheless, he was listed as producer on the cassette-only EP.

It was Club Detroit's Rob Douglas, according to Connelly, who convinced the rock legend to hire the Headlights to play behind him on his 1991 "comeback" tour (the Byrds had just been inducted into the Rock and Roll Hall of Fame).

"You've got the perfect backup band in your back yard," Douglas said. "They play the Byrds, they play jangle-rock, they're your perfect band."

The tour was a success, and the Headlights even appeared on the *Tonight Show* with McGuinn.

However, says Connelly, he never saw that exposure, the stops in L.A. and New York, as a "big break" for the Headlights. "Everyone," he smirks, "was making such a big deal out of it. But I knew we were just a glorified backup band."

In short order, McGuinn moved on and the Headlights were back playing the Masquerade, Clancy's, Club Detroit and the ACL Club.

Even though they were feted as the "local boys made good," Connelly – an admitted homebody – was only too glad to be back in local clubs. He was all into the big fish, small pond equation.

"I didn't have that drive, that desire to be famous," he says. "I wanted to be accepted, and I wanted to be loved and all, but I didn't care about the music business."

It all started, improbably, with a band that played nothing but Grateful Dead covers. Connelly was the singer and guitarist for the group, which was called Real Eyes (aka Realize).

In 1972, at a Battle of the Bands contest in Tampa, he met folksinger Charlotte Wilson. They both won in their respective categories, and not so long afterwards they became an item.

With violinist Paul Kelly, Connelly and Wilson formed an acoustic group, Just Another Rainbow. "We were like a high-energy Old and in the Way," recalls Connelly, "a high-energy bluegrass band. We played the Dead, New Riders ... with two Martin guitars and a fiddle."

In time the band added a bass-playing friend of Connelly's younger brother named Scott Dempster, and drummer Bob Leichner.

Just Another Rainbow was the first band to perform live in the WYNF Studios when the station began in 1979, and the first to play Skippers Smokehouse when it opened the following year.

But a change was coming.

"When new wave hit, I got totally enamored with it," Connelly says. "So we became a schizophrenic band, because we all got into this stuff, but still our power base was this country-rock thing." They'd do country-rock for the first set, "but for the second set we'd come out and do Elvis Costello, Nick Lowe, Blondie … the first and second set were two completely different bands. It was kinda weird, but people accepted it."

As a moniker, Just Another Rainbow was colossally uncool. An early manager suggested The Headlites … the spelling was eventually changed to the significantly less cutesy Headlights.

By the time Steve and Charlotte's relationship soured, in 1980, the old country-rock stuff was gone, as was the fiddler. They were a full time new wave rock 'n' roll group. Her replacement as singer and second guitarist was Steve Robinson, an Englishman recently arrived in the bay area. And the band's music continued to evolve.

Robinson, also a strong singer and songwriter, took the band on a deeper dive into modern English sounds – the likes of Echo & the Bunnymen, U2, XTC and the Smiths.

The longest-lived, "classic" band was Connelly and Robinson on guitars (electric and acoustic, respectively) and vocals, Dempster on bass and Danny DiPietra playing drums.

"After I began to write songs," recalls Robinson, "I think I had more of an effect on the band than in those early days. Although Steve and I didn't verbalize it, I think that over time, our songwriting styles maybe had a bit of a symbiotic thing going on. I was certainly influenced by him, and I think that in some way, some of what I brought to the table rubbed off on him, and The Headlights gained a little focus and an identity of their own."

Next, the great Roger McGuinn adventure – when the Byrd and the band played *Tonight* (with then-guest host Jay Leno) in April, 1991, VCRs all over Tampa Bay were set on record. But by '94, everyone was out of gas. The Headlights disbanded, and the musicians went their separate ways.

In 1995 Connelly signed on as Chief Engineer at Zen, a small Pinellas County recording studio. Eventually he bought the business, and produced (and played on) dozens of records by local artists, including some by former Headlights.

"Our recorded output is woefully inadequate," Robinson says today. "I think it weighed on us all. Even after the band broke up, we'd often speak of getting together to record some new Headlights material. We even did assemble once at Zen (at Scott's behest, of course) and laid down rhythm tracks for a couple of songs, but sadly, we never finished work on them.

"It's a shame, because I remember it being a great time and a few musical sparks were flying. Personally, I felt like we had a pretty damn good album left in us, so I feel a little sad that we didn't follow

through."

A liver transplant in 2015 slowed Connelly down – a little – and the loss of studio business due to Covid-19 meant he was forced to sell his interest in Zen. But no matter: "It's good, I'm enjoying it," he says. "I made six records in my front room last year with just one microphone, a pre-amp, a drum machine and a guitar box."

In November 2022 Scott Dempster died of a heart attack, at age 67. "Scott loved being in a band more than anyone I've ever known," Robinson says. "It was just in his soul, and he had an energy about him when it came to getting the lacs together for rehearsals, recording anc playing shows. He was the engine room of the band really; always the one putting in the legwork to make things happen for us."

Acknowledgements

Thanks a million Roger Prinse, Faune Walker, Bobby Salerno, Michelle Middleton Allen, John Allen, Bridget Burke, Jim Swallow, Jessy Breckinridge, Rui Farias, Yolanda Fernandez, Kelsey Long, David Yates, Kiley Diaz, Dick Crippen, Mike Clark, Lisa Johnson Marone, Chris Skillman, Anne Field, Amy Kagan and Patty Ware. Much gratitude to Isa Crosta and Amy Cianci.

For Riley.

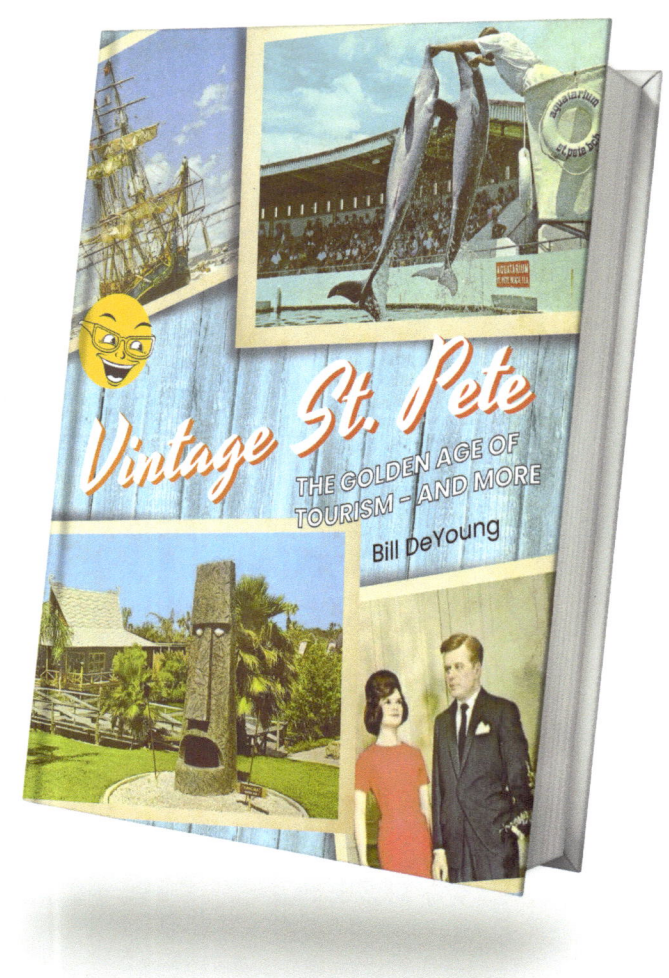

Vintage St. Pete:
The Golden Age of Tourism – and More

Sunken Gardens – Webb's City – Marine Area/John's Pass Aquarium- Tiki Gardens – London Wax Museum – The Aquatarium – MGM's Bounty- The Pier – Capone, the Babe & the Gangplank – The Earl Gresh Wood Parade - Fort DeSoto & Fort Dade – Marilyn Monroe & Joe DiMaggio – Ralph Heath's Suncoast Seabird Sanctuary – Dr. Paul Bearer – The Manhattan Casino - The Operetta & the Music Circus – The Bayfront Center – Gay Blades Roller Rink – Boyd Hill Nature Trail Zoo – Making Movies on Weedon Island – Making 'HEALTH' – Making 'Cocoon'

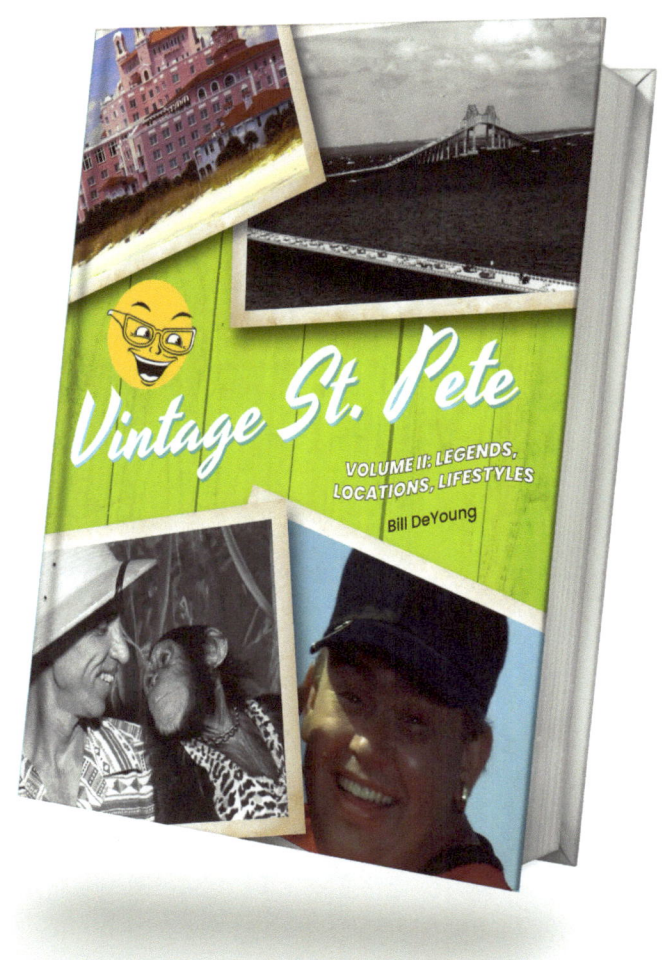

Vintage St. Pete Volume II: Legends, Locations, Lifestyles

Tony Jannus and his Flight into History – The Vinoy Park Hotel – The Don CeSar - George Snow Hill at Pass-a-Grille - Raising the Sunshine Skyway Bridge - Captain Mac – 'Abraham, Martin & John, the St. Pete Connection – Soup, soap & snake oil: John 3:16 Cook – From Bogart to Brad Pitt – Filming 'Route 66' – Bob Dylan's TV special – Making 'Summer Rental' – Tom Petty, MTV & the Don - The Beach Theatre – The Playhouse Theatre- Haslam's Books - The Florida Wild Animal Ranch – The Royal Theatre – 'Florida Aflame' – The Richest Man in the World - Celebrity Dinner Theaters – Our Lady of Clearwater

About the author

Bill DeYoung is the author of two previous *Vintage St. Pete* books. He is a St. Petersburg native and a veteran Florida journalist. Other titles include *Skyway: The True Story of Tampa Bay's Signature Bridge and the Man Who Brought it Down* and *Phil Gernhard Record Man* (University Press of Florida), and *I Need to Know: The Lost Music Interviews* (St. Petersburg Press).